Psychological Approaches to Dermatology

Psychological Approaches to Dermatology

Linda Papadopoulos
Robert Bor

With dermatological advice from Professor John Hawk

BPS BOOKS   THE BRITISH
PSYCHOLOGICAL
SOCIETY

First published in 1999 by BPS Books (The British Psychological Society), St Andrews House, 48 Princess Road East, Leicester LE1 7DR, UK.

A catalogue record for this book is available from the British Library.

Library of Congress Cataloguing-in-Publication Data on file.

ISBN 1 85433 292 9

Typeset by Book Production Services, London.
Printed in Great Britain by MPG Books Limited

About the authors

Linda Papadopoulos is a Senior Lecturer in Counselling Psychology at London Guildhall University. She studied at York University in Toronto, Canada and received her counselling training at the City University in London. She is a Chartered Counselling and Health Psychologist and has published widely in the field of medical psychology and psychocutaneous disease and runs specialist courses in counselling people with disfigurement. She has worked in numerous health psychology and primary care settings and runs workshops with medical students on the psychological implications of illness.

Robert Bor is Professor of Psychology at London Guildhall University, and a Chartered Clinical, Counselling and Health Psychologist. He trained in the practice and teaching of family therapy at the Tavistock Clinic, is a member of the Tavistock Society of Psychotherapists and is a UKCP Registered Systemic Therapist. He is a clinical member of the Institute of Family Therapy, a member of the American Family Therapy Academy and the American Association for Marriage and Family Therapy. He works in hospital, community and primary care settings, and extensively with acute and chronically ill patients and their families. He acts as a consultant to medical and nursing colleagues and teaches communication skills to medical students. He has published widely on the impact of illness in families and serves on the editorial board of numerous international journals. He also has an interest in aviation psychology and is a qualified pilot. He is a Churchill Fellow.

Professor John L.M. Hawk is a Consultant Dermatologist at the St John's Institute of Dermatology at St. Thomas's Hospital in London. He has published extensively in the field of dermatology and is the chief editor of the journal *Clinical and Experimental Dermatology*. He serves on numerous medical advisory committees and has an interest in the field of psychodermatology. He is a leading figure in the area of pigmentation disorders of the skin.

Acknowlegements

We are specially grateful to Professor Finlay for allowing us to reproduce his questionnaires and providing us with an invaluable resource for both practitoners and clinicians. Thanks also go to Dr Charles Legg for his advice on research in psychodermatology, The Vitiligo Society and the Disfigurement Guidance Center for providing advice and sensitive insight into the issues faced by people with skin disease, and to Joyce Collins and Rachel Gear for their constant support and encouragement. Finally we would like to thank our patients for sharing their experiences in counselling and therapy, and inspiring us to explore the area of counselling in dermatology.

Dedications

L.P: *To my wonderful parents for their unwavering and unconditional love and support, to Alexia for inspiring me, and above all, to my husband Teddy for everything.*

R.B: *To my father Simon who has taught me the most about dermatology.*

Contents

Foreword

The connection between skin disease and any psychological basis for its induction or continuation has always been a controversial issue. What is less contentious however is the recognition that there is a high psychological morbidity among many dermatology patients and that their physicians have not always had good access to psychological support services for their patients. Further, there has been little real evaluation of change of the situation over the years, at least until very recently with the arrival of Linda Papadopoulos and Robert Bor on the scene. These two extremely competent and energetic individuals have now looked into the true relationship between the psyche and skin disease from all points of view and it now seems very likely that clear connections are often present.

This book therefore fills a gap in the literature on patient care in dermatology. Not only do the authors succinctly present the recent available evidence from medical and psychological research, but they also discuss the importance of providing effective psychological support in the dermatology clinic and in general medical practice. They further describe how psychological support and advice, as well as innovative psychotherapeutic techniques, can improve skin disease and enable patients to cope with it better, and they make a very strong case for a much closer relationship between dermatology and psychology. The quest for greater collaboration between the specialties is modelled in very practical descriptions of complex psychological and counselling approaches, and dermatologists, general practitioners, nurses, physiotherapists, students and other health care professionals will certainly find a wealth of information and practical hints in this book on how to communicate with their patients about sensitive and at times distressing topics. Psychologists, counsellors, psychotherapists and others who provide expert psychological support for patients will also learn about the application of their skills to the problems experienced by dermatology patients and by those who work in dermatology settings.

I am delighted to have been able to contribute just a little to this splendid book by providing some dermatological advice. I feel that this book should now help remove forever many of the mysteries previously surrounding the relationship between skin disease and the psyche. I very much wish the work the major success it deserves.

Professor John Hawk,
St John's Institute of Dermatology, St Thomas's Hospital, London

1

Introduction

The skin has been referred to as the organ of expression, and as the largest and most superficial organ of the body, it serves as the major boundary between ourselves and the outside world. It acts as the surface of contact between us and our environment. It defines our limits and often provides a window to internal somatic and psychological processes. Its capacity to react to physical and psychological stimuli (e.g. a rash from infection or blushing when we are shy or embarrassed) suggests that it is a complex organ, which affects and is affected by both physical and psychological stimuli.

Although only seldom life threatening, skin problems and disease may be evident to others because they affect and alter physical appearance. The consequences of this are twofold. Firstly, the visibility or prominence of the disease may attract attention in social situations, thus preventing the person from keeping a skin condition private or personal. Furthermore, some people associate skin disease with contagion or lack of hygiene, and therefore sufferers may also find that others react negatively towards them, or treat them differently because of their appearance. Secondly, the physical changes that may result from skin disease can have a negative effect on a person's **body image**, and high levels of psychological morbidity are often associated with this. The person may thus feel stigmatized and avoid certain social situations. Those who suffer from dermatological conditions have been found to experience higher levels of distress and anxiety, reduced self-esteem and body image disturbance than those who are unaffected and in extreme cases this can even lead to suicide in the sufferer.

The primary aim of this book is to describe how skin disease can affect a person's self-identity and relationships with others. It also aims to consider the relevance of psychological factors in the onset and treatment of skin disease, with a main emphasis on how psychological counselling can help the affected individual. This book is designed to serve as guide for those who work in the field of dermatology as well as other health care professionals such as doctors, nurses, physiotherapists, psychologists, psychotherapists, counsellors and social workers thereby leading to an understanding of patients' psychological reactions to their conditions. Although most health professionals who work in dermatology settings consider the psychological consequences of skin problems for their patients, limited psychological support is usually provided within the confines of busy clinics and dwindling resources, and some professionals feel inadequately trained for this task. Consequently, psychological support and care may be secondary to the medical interventions and treatment that patients receive. However, effective psychological counselling can improve clinical treatment and outcomes, enhance communication in the doctor–nurse–patient relationship and help patients and their families to cope better with bad news and unwelcome circumstances. This book describes how health care professionals can use counselling skills to help dermatology patients cope with a broad range of psychosocial consequences of their condition. It is also hoped that by understanding more about the experiences of patients who live with skin conditions, the reader will gain some insight into the way that these conditions affect peoples' lives.

We anticipate that those reading this book will have different levels of training and experience in psychological therapies. Doctors and nurses who work with patients, but whose training and practice is more clinically orientated, may want to expand their understanding of how these conditions affect patients' lives psychologically and also develop their counselling skills so as to offer their patients more holistic and psychologically minded care. Counsellors, psychologists and social workers, who have specialist training in counselling and psychotherapeutic skills, will be able to increase their understanding of the specific problems that dermatology patients face and how to help patients cope with these problems. Finally, people with skin conditions, as well as their friends and family members, may be keen to understand more about the relationship between psychology and dermatology, and the mind–body connection in relation to the onset, maintenance and treatment of skin problems. Our aim is to describe psychological processes associated with dermatological problems.

How common are skin problems?

Unlike conditions such as cancer and human immunodeficiency virus (HIV) disease, which are ranked high on the list of medical problems in terms of public awareness, dermatological conditions rarely receive attention in public health campaigns and consequently their effect on peoples' lives tends to be underrated. It is estimated that approximately 20% of the UK population suffer with some form of skin disease at any given time, with eczema, acne and infectious disorders (e.g. athlete's foot) being the most commonly presenting complaints to general practitioners (GPs) and dermatologists. Approximately 15–20% of a GP's workload and 6% of hospital out-patient referrals are for skin problems. Skin disease too is the most frequent reason for sick leave from work and is the most common industrial disease (Gawkrodger, 1997). It may also be symptomatic of other medical conditions. Kaposi's sarcoma, for example, is sometimes associated with HIV disease while skin tumours may result from the neurological condition neurofibromatosis. Where the skin condition is a symptom of another illness, it is seen to be a part of a systemic problem or condition. Skin problems can also be **iatrogenic**, that is caused by the treatment of other medical conditions. An example of this is a skin rash that develops or erupts after a patient is prescribed medication for another problem

Lay views on skin disease

Skin disease, as is the case with most other medical conditions that alter physical appearance, was viewed in the past as a form of punishment. People have also explained it in terms of 'payment' for a 'wrongdoing' of either the sufferer or their family. This view that a karmic force may be responsible for punishing 'bad' people with some sort of deformity or illness dates back thousands of years. Thus in many parts of the world, birthmarks, especially hairy ones, have been considered the result of a woman having engaged in intimate contact with the devil or a wild animal (Shaw, 1981). Again, in some parts of Africa, children born with **albinism** are seen as having been touched by an evil spirit or punished as the result of their mother's having been unfaithful to her husband by sleeping with a white man. The stigmatizing nature of conditions such as leprosy have their roots in the belief that sufferers are unclean, contagious or unable to care for themselves. People with skin diseases have historically been treated as second-class citizens, avoided, pitied and shunned.

These negative reactions towards people who suffered with some form of skin condition were born out of the belief that they were in some way responsible for their misfortune. Stigmatization is associated with many forms of disfigurement and is sometimes underscored by popular images portrayed in literature and in the media. From fairy tales to soap operas, villains are generally depicted as having not only deviant personalities, but also 'deviant' physical characteristics. Heroes on the other hand, are often portrayed as flawless and beautiful.

It is important to note that, while in the majority of cases negative attributes tend to be associated with visible skin conditions, there have been some cases where the opposite is true. In certain tribes, for example, a child born with albinism may be regarded as having special divine powers and therefore respected and revered by those around them. There is also the case of the 'Select Knights of St John', a group of elite swordsmen and warriors whose members all had red birthmarks on their faces; this birthmark was thought to signify strength and bravery, and membership of the order was open only to those who had been 'blessed' with the mark. Cases such as these are rare however, and the majority of those whose physical appearance is significantly different from the norm more commonly face fear, ignorance and misunderstanding from those around them.

Although erroneous beliefs about the causes of skin conditions are now less common, misconceptions and myths still abound about many of them. These are often related to the typology of the skin condition (this is discussed in detail in Chapter 2). For example, acne is sometimes associated with immaturity or lack of personal hygiene. Reactions from others may range from pity to disgust. Other conditions, such as HIV-associated Kaposi's sarcoma may instead evoke ideas about a person's sexuality or morality. Reactions to skin conditions develop out of beliefs about:

- how the person developed the condition
- the course it will take (progressive, episodic)
- whether it is treatable
- prevailing views/stereotypes about it
- its location, colour, size or shape
- one's relationship to the affected person.

Perceptions of sufferers

Because skin diseases are often visible to others, sufferers may be more prone to the social and emotional consequences of their condition. However, psychological factors are sometimes overlooked or ignored by health practitioners because most skin problems are not regarded as serious or life threatening, even though non-life threatening skin conditions (such as acne) can adversely affect a person's well-being and self-esteem. Dermatological problems are often not recognized as a handicap in the general population and people with skin conditions may also suffer the added problem of trivialization of their distress, which can further exacerbate the intensity or seriousness of feelings associated with their condition. Box 1.1 outlines some common misconceptions held about dermatology patients.

Box 1.1   *Common misconceptions regarding skin disease*

- Because most skin conditions are not life threatening, these do not pose a significant problem for the patient.
- If the condition is not physically handicapping, then the person's activities and daily routine will not be affected.
- The perceived severity of the condition and its psychosocial consequences are directly related.
- Every person with a skin condition is affected in the same way regardless of age, gender or race.
- No variation exists with regard to how people react to different skin conditions.

The role of counselling

We have briefly reviewed how people with skin problems may be affected by their condition. It is helpful to consider how psychological counselling can address and respond to some of these issues. In recent years, health care professionals have recognized that people with medical conditions and their families can be helped through psychological counselling to cope better with chronic or acute illness (Bor et al., 1998). Counselling refers to and involves the work of all health professionals, and indeed non-professionals, who come in contact with patients. Focused counselling in health care settings and for people with medical conditions can specifically:

- improve the person's understanding of the problem
- address their concerns
- address the family's concerns
- help them to cope better
- improve compliance with treatment
- reduce psychological morbidity
- reduce over-reliance on medical and nursing care.

Psychological counselling can also provide an environment in which patients' feelings and anxieties can be explored. It can empower patients to address their concerns about their illnesses, identify useful coping techniques and develop new ones. Counselling can also help patients make sense of their condition since many skin conditions have an uncertain etiology and patients may construct personal accounts to 'explain' their condition. Some of these may have a detrimental affect on adjustment, depending on the nature of patients' beliefs. This was the case with a 53–year-old female vitiligo patient who first developed the condition around her genitalia when she was 11 years old. She had first noticed the condition following an unwanted sexual encounter with one of her classmates. Since the onset of the condition followed the sexual encounter, she was convinced that the condition was brought on as a consequence of sexual contact. This resulted in her feeling ashamed and avoiding sexual contact in later life. Box 1.2 is a section of a transcript from a counselling session where this patient describes her story.

Box 1.2 Adjustment and causal attributions in skin disease

'I was convinced that I was being punished for having had a sexual encounter with that boy. I was sure that whoever saw my patches would know that I had contracted some sort of venereal disease, that I was dirty. I have always believed, and part of me still does, that I was to blame for it, and that the white patches are there for everyone to know that I have done something dirty. I haven't been able to wear short sleeves, skirts or anything that would reveal my patches for the last 40 years because every time I look down at my vitiligo I feel guilty and ashamed.'

Counselling can also help to normalize a patient's feelings. Dermatology patients may be referred for counselling because they convey directly or indirectly to doctors or nurses that they find it difficult to cope with their condition. Feelings of sadness or guilt about not being able to deal with something that others may view as trivial may prompt a referral for counselling which in turn can help to provide both practical methods for coping with the effects of skin disease and a safe environment where patients can explore their feelings.

The effects of skin conditions usually permeate much deeper than the skin. The association with contagion and lack of hygiene makes these conditions socially stigmatizing and therefore patients may be susceptible to the negative reactions of those around them (see Chapter 5). Depending on a range of factors, from the type of skin condition to provision and availability of social support, the psychological effects of skin disease can range from minimal to devastating.

About the book

The main focus of this book is to describe:

• the psychological impact of dermatological conditions
• the effects of skin disease on social and familial relationships

- how to recognize psychological problems associated with skin disease
- the use of psychological counselling with dermatology patients.

As medicine becomes more consumer-orientated, health care professionals are likely to feel the need to develop a greater understanding of the emotional needs of their patients and how best to respond to them. Communication skills between health professionals and their patients are highly relevant in this regard (Lloyd and Bor, 1996). In the field of dermatology, where different conditions may have a serious psychological impact on the person, how professionals engage with their patients is especially important. There is, of course, a difference between being a professional counsellor and having counselling skills. This book is aimed primarily at those who work with dermatology patients in a medical capacity but feel that they do not have the specialist knowledge to counsel their patients; it is aimed as well at psychologists, counsellors and psychotherapists who may be unaccustomed to working with people who have medical problems or who have little experience of working with dermatology patients. This book attempts to convey an approach to counselling for dermatological problems that can be applied to, and developed within, various clinical settings and to a range of clinical problems.

This chapter has sought to provide a brief overview of the psychological consequences of living with a skin disease, and has outlined some common misconceptions and lay views held about dermatology patients. We have also introduced the role of counselling in helping patients with skin disease. Chapter 2 describes how different skin conditions affect a person's adjustment to their illness. A description of some of the most common conditions, their course and treatment, is given and myths which exist about particular disorders are discussed. Issues covered in Chapter 3 centre around coping and adapting to skin problems including how patients perceive changes in their appearance and how these affect their psychosocial functioning. The reciprocal relationship between the skin and the psyche is examined in Chapter 4 and we also undertake an exploration of how psychological factors can influence the onset and progression of various skin conditions. Chapter 5 takes an in-depth look at the psychosocial consequences of skin disease, focusing on the way that body image, self-esteem and quality of life are affected with the onset of a cutaneous condition. This leads to a discussion of how different relationships are affected by the onset of skin disease (Chapter 6). Chapter 7 introduces some basic concepts about counselling and how these can be applied to the unique issues faced by dermatology patients. Chapter 8 describes some conceptual ideas about counselling in health care settings. Chapter 9 builds on the previous two chapters and outlines more advanced theoretical and practical ideas relating to counselling. In Chapter 10 we

7

explore the challenge of counselling patients with psychosomatic illness related to dermatology, and in Chapter 11 the discussion centres on working with children and parents. Finally, Chapter 12 describes issues that arise in working within a multi-disciplinary team, and suggestions are made for achieving effective collaborative relationships between professionals.

Our hope is that, as well as providing ideas about how to counsel dermatology patients, the contents of this book will also convey an understanding of how dermatology patients are affected by their condition and the mind–body connection in the treatment of skin disease.

2

Typology of Skin Problems

Introduction

In this chapter we consider how the typology of different skin conditions (i.e. their nature, onset, course and appearance) can affect how people adapt to and cope with their skin problem. Depending on when and how a person develops a particular skin problem they will have to face specific adaptation tasks and cope with specific challenges. In the case of congenital cutaneous conditions for example, early social experiences will generally be affected by a person's appearance. It has been suggested that strangers looking into the pram of a child with a deformity withhold smiles and reinforcing gestures until they have adjusted to the initial shock of the baby's appearance (Field and Vega-Lahr, 1984). Mothers of infants with a disfiguring skin condition often find it difficult to smile or communicate positively with the child if they feel unsettled by their child's appearance. As the child grows up, he or she may begin to notice ambivalent reactions of others towards their appearance. Other children may be curious, rejecting or overtly cruel, and the child with an obvious cutaneous condition may grow up with an awareness of being different. The child may become reserved, quiet, withdrawn or non-competitive, or try to compensate for the disfigurement by over-achieving at school or at sports (Partridge 1994; Timberlake, 1985). On the other hand people who acquire a visible skin disease later on in life are faced with different adaptation tasks than those with congenital skin conditions, particularly if it is on the face and hands. A disfiguring skin disease can adversely affect body image, confidence and, in certain instances, a person's overall quality of life.

Typology of skin disease

As is the case with most illnesses the manner in which a skin disease is acquired, and the course it will run, can significantly affect a person's adjustment to their condition. There are three broad categories under which skin diseases fall in terms of their course, namely, progressive, episodic and acute. These are now discussed.

Progressive

Conditions that fall under this category have a known course. Conditions such as melanomas come under this heading. If left untreated, melanomas will get progressively worse and in some cases cause death. The course that progressive conditions follow can have both positive and negative aspects in terms of patients' psychological adjustment to the condition. On the one hand, because the condition will progress in a predictable fashion, patients should know what to expect and be able to prepare for it. On the other hand, however, the course that the condition will be expected to take is usually based on general estimates and may vary from patient to patient. It may therefore cause anxiety if the condition does not progress as the patient expects.

Episodic

Episodic conditions fluctuate between periods of exacerbation and dormancy. In this case, anxiety will be caused not only by the frequency of fluctuations between deterioration and stability but also by the uncertainty of not knowing when these fluctuations will occur. These episodes may be dependent upon specific environmental or behavioural factors, but may also appear to fluctuate at random. This will have implications for how the patient copes with their condition and feelings of control over the condition.

Acute

Conditions that are deemed to be acute tend to be short-lived and follow a predictable course. These conditions require the patient to act quickly making the necessary practical and affective changes to facilitate the healing process. From a psychological perspective, because of the transitory nature of acute conditions, they may have no significant effect on the sufferer. In some cases however, the social significance of acute conditions can have a lasting effect on the patient. This may be particularly relevant, for example, in dermatovenereological conditions such as gonorrhoea and syphilis.

Causes of skin disease

As well as differing in terms of their course, skin conditions also differ in terms of their onset. There are two main types of onset, namely congenital and acquired.

Congenital

Conditions that are present at birth are usually the result of genetic inheritance and include congenital vascular defects, congenital naevi, and albinism. Some of the conditions which fall under this category may occur in brief episodes, may be treatable and require little adaptation from the affected individual. Other conditions, such as vascular disorders, may remain with the patient throughout life and therefore require more long-term adaptation. In the case of most conditions which fall under this category, the parents may be more affected initially than the infant child. The way that parents cope with their child's condition will inevitably affect how the child will cope and adapt to it (this is discussed in detail in Chapter 11).

Acquired

Conditions which fall under this category may be either a symptom of another condition, as in the case of Immunodeficiency and AIDS-related Kaposi's sarcoma, or a condition in and of itself, for example melanoma. In the former, patients have to contend with various issues including the possibility of a reduced life expectancy, physical handicap and altered appearance. Anecdotal reports suggest that people with life threatening conditions which have a disfiguring component are often as concerned about their altered appearance as they are about their deteriorating health. Therefore, the assumption that the impact of the disfiguring nature of certain conditions is lessened or overshadowed by the physical significance may not be valid. In the latter case, the focus tends to be on the condition, its progression, appearance, distribution and symptoms. The patient may become obsessed with the shape and size of their lesions and engage in frequent checking behaviours to see if these have changed. Since many skin conditions have an unknown aetiology, the patient may construct beliefs surrounding aetiology and progression, and may in turn engage in 'superstitious' behaviours to gain control over the condition. For example, someone who developed psoriasis after using a public swimming pool may avoid any form of swimming for fear that that the condition will get worse.

Other factors that can influence adjustment

The size, contour and location of a lesion or patch of diseased skin may also determine how the condition affects the patient's life. If the lesions are on the torso, then the person may avoid activities such as swimming and others which may involve exposure of the body. Alternatively, if the lesions are on the face, then the person may have to become accustomed to wearing camouflage make-up or avoid some social activities.

Common skin conditions

The discussion so far suggests that it is important that health professionals have a clear understanding of the physical symptoms that our patients experience and the way that these can affect psychosocial functioning. Skin conditions are by no means rare. However, since little attention is paid to examining the way that these conditions affect patients' lives from a psychosocial perspective, many patients are left on their own to cope with and understand the psychological implications of their condition. This may lead to negative or erroneous beliefs about their condition and the effect that it has on them. Some of the most common skin conditions, their incidence in the general population and treatments are outlined in Boxes 2.1 to 2.6. For further details refer to C.K. Bridgett (1996) or E. Bondi (1991).

Box 2.1 Acne

Definition: a chronic inflammation of the pilosebaceous glands (hair follicles that contain large oil-producing cells) of the face, upper arms and upper chest. Lesions over the follicles, which become blocked by oil, may appear as solid elevations of the skin (**papules**), as pus-filled blisters (**pustules**), as **cysts** or as scars. Clinical variants of the condition include *acne conglobata* – this is the most severe form in which large nodules and cysts rupture under the skin leaving scars; *acne cosmetica* – a mild non-inflammatory form of the condition often triggered by acnegenic cosmetics; *actinic acne* – which is rare and occurs following exposure to sunlight; *acne excorie* – a form seen more frequently in females, where lesions tend to be superficial; and the *usual acne vulgaris* – where a variety of lesions may be present, ranging from blackheads and whiteheads to inflamed **nodules** and cysts depending on the severity.

Distribution and severity: common sites of involvement include the face, neck, shoulders, chest and back. The severity of acne depends on its extent and the type of lesion, with cysts being the most damaging. In many cases long-term scarring can result.

Prevalence: Acne vulgaris is one of the most common skin conditions, occurring, usually temporarily, in more than 80% of the

---

population in some form. Acne affects males and females equally and the age of onset is usually early puberty, with persistence often into the early twenties (Bondi et al., 1991).

Cause: three general mechanisms have been put forward as causing acne: (i) excessive sebum production or seborrhoea; (ii) abnormal shedding of the epithelial cells that line the follicles; (iii) a bacterium often initiated by the hormonal increases of adolescence known as propionibacterium acnes, which proliferates in the follicles as a consequence of the increased sebum.

Treatment depends on the type and extent of the acne. 'Over-the-counter creams' and topical treatment are usually effective for mild acne and a combination of varying strengths of antibiotics and topical treatments are used for more severe cases.

Box 2.2 Eczema

Definition: eczema is a pruritic inflammation of the skin frequently seen in association with the allergic conditions asthma and hay fever. It is characterized by moist red weeping skin during the acute stages and dry, scaly skin in its more chronic forms.

Distribution: most commonly affects face and knee and elbow flexures.

Prevalence: approximately 12–15% of infants are affected by the so-called **atopic** forms of this condition. It usually starts within the first six months of life. Remission occurs by age 15 in up to 75% of cases, although some patients may relapse later. The commonest manifestation in adult life is hand or foot dermatitis. However, a small percentage of adults have a chronic severe form of the condition, which then may be exacerbated by exposure to irritants such as dust and chemicals.

Cause: there is a genetic component to the condition with around 70% of patients having a family history of eczema, asthma or hay fever. The cause is thought to be related to an imbalance in immune function, including defective T-cell function, and is probably essentially a form of excessive or allergic response to environmental substances such as house dust or pityrosporum yeast present on the skin.

Treatment: specific treatments for eczema include emollients, topical steroids, oral antihistamines, oral antibiotics and PUVA therapy (a combination of psoralens and exposure to UVA light). General measures in the management of the condition also include wearing loose cotton clothing, keeping nails short in order to avoid injury from scratching, and keeping the patient away from house pets and dust, which can exacerbate the condition in atopic patients.

Box 2.3 Vitiligo

Definition: vitiligo is an acquired disorder resulting in the occurrence of white non-scaly lesions. At the affected sites, the hair also usually loses its colour. The course of the condition is unpredictable, some areas perhaps remaining unaffected for years, others completely losing their pigmentation within few weeks.

Distribution: loss of pigmentation can occur anywhere on the body's surface but commonly on knees, elbows, hips, nipples, genital area, hands and feet. The condition can be distributed symmetrically where lesions take the same form on either side of the body, non-symmetrically where there is no clear pattern, focally where only a few well defined lesions are apparent or universally where most of the pigmentation has been lost.

Prevalence: vitiligo affects approximately 1% of the population of all races. Males and females are affected equally and the age of onset is commonly somewhere between 10 and 30 years.

Cause: no clear etiology for the condition exists although a genetically determined **autoimmune** basis is thought to be implicated since vitiligo has a higher than normal comorbidity with conditions such as pernicious anaemia, thyroid disease and Addison's disease.

Treatment: unfortunately, there is no reliably effective treatment for this condition. Topical steroid treatment to the small areas and courses of oral psoralen therapy in conjunction with UVA radiation exposure (PUVA) over many months are the most common therapies offered and, failing this, patients are usually advised to use camouflage make-up to conceal the lesions. In cases where lesions cover the majority of the body, however, complete depigmentation using hydroquinone may be considered.

Box 2.4 Psoriasis

Definition: psoriasis is a chronic inflammatory skin condition, characterized by localized, widespread well-demarcated red plaques often topped by silvery scales. In 10% of cases psoriasis is associated with a degree of arthritis.

Distribution: areas most commonly affected are the elbows, knees and scalp. The disease often persists throughout life frequently displaying a tendency for improvement in the summer.

Prevalence: psoriasis affects approximately 2% of the population in Europe and North America but may be less common in Africa and Japan. Males and females are affected equally. Onset can occur at any age, but is most common in the second and third decades of life. It rarely occurs in children under 8 years of age. A familial tendency for the condition has been noted in around 40% of cases.

Cause: although the exact cause of psoriasis is not fully understood, the basic abnormality is thought to be immunologically based, perhaps autoimmune, and is associated with an enlarged population of epidermal cells that divide too rapidly. The epidermal cell proliferation is increased by 20 times or more in psoriatic as compared to normal skin.

Treatment: the selected treatment depends upon the degree of rash, the site of the lesions and the pattern of distribution. Thus mild forms of the condition tend to be treated with topical corticosteroids, in more severe cases this therapy being augmented by other topical treatments such as tars. In severe cases, topical therapy may be combined with phototherapy or PUVA, or with oral immunosuppressive therapy.

Box 2.5 Port-wine stains (naevus flammeus)

Definition and distribution: this is a congenital condition which presents as a flat irregular red or purple lesion. There are two types of port-wine stain: medially located **naevi**, occurring as faint red lesions over the scalp, nape of neck or centre of face which tend to remain flat throughout the patient's life and become less prominent over time; laterally located naevi on the

15

other hand are usually seen unilaterally over the face but may also occur on the extremities; these begin as red and flat lesions but over time can change to purple and become more papular, persisting throughout life and becoming more prominent.

Cause: although there is no clear causal mechanism for this condition, port-wine stains are associated with a dilation or proliferation of cutaneous blood vessels.

Treatment: port-wine stains can be concealed with camouflage make-up although laser treatment is increasingly available, which can often obliterate the abnormal dermal vessels over a course of treatment.

Box 2.6 Malignant melanoma

Definition and distribution: malignant melanoma is a tumour of the melanocytes or tanning cells, resulting from the malignant transformation of these epidermal cells; it is the most lethal type of skin tumour. There are four main variants of this condition. Superficial spreading malignant melanoma is the most common type accounting for 50% of all cases seen in the UK. A higher proportion of females than males is affected and the condition is most commonly seen on the lower leg. Lentigo malignant melanoma accounts for 15% of UK cases and arises in clearly sun-damaged skin, most commonly affecting the face and arms. Acral lentiginous malignant melanoma makes up only 10% of cases in the UK, affecting the palms, soles and nail beds. It is often diagnosed too late and has a poor survival rate. Finally, nodular malignant melanoma is seen in 25% of British cases and is more common in males; in this variety, hyperpigmented lesions grow rapidly, producing ulcers.

Prevalence: the prevalence of melanoma is around 0.0001%, that is one in every 10,000. However, the incidence is rapidly rising and nearly doubles every decade. It also presents at a younger age in both sexes. This is probably because of lifestyle changes, such as the increased popularity of sunny holidays and cosmetic tanning. It occurs in all races but mostly in fair-skinned populations, and in Britain women are affected twice as frequently as men. Males tend to develop the condition most commonly on their backs, females most frequently on the lower leg.

Cause: the exact cause of malignant melanoma is not known, but circumstantial evidence strongly suggests that intermittent, heavy exposure to sunlight is the main factor in its development. Other risk factors include having a family member with the condition, having multiple (>100) naevi, and burning easily in the sun.

Treatment: the main treatment is surgical removal, a skin graft often being necessary; it is frequently fatal if treated late and a positive outcome is closely linked to early detection and treatment.

Skin disorders of a psychogenic origin

There is evidence to suggest that certain skin conditions can be triggered by a person's psychological state. In addition, there are certain skin conditions, such as dermatitis artefacta and neurotic **excoriations**, which are believed to have a psychological aetiology. These disorders are at the extreme end of the psychodermatology spectrum, and patients who present with these may fall under the category of the 'worried well'. They often insist that their problems are medical and resist a psychological explanation for them. Since the skin is the most accessible organ of the body, patients may also scratch, pinch or manipulate their skin in such a way that it appears to be abnormal. Patients who present to GPs or dermatologists with these conditions may do so because it is easier for them to admit to having a physical problem rather than a psychological one. Treatment of these conditions requires close collaboration between doctors, nurses, psychologists and psychiatrists. In many cases, patients resist referral for psychological treatment because they tend to regard their problem as medical, if they seek specialist help at all. A detailed discussion of how counselling skills can be used when working with patients in this category is outlined in Chapter 10. Table 2.1 outlines certain known skin conditions of psychogenic origin.

Typology and stigma

The extent to which a patient will feel stigmatized may often depend on the nature of the skin condition and beliefs associated with it. In their study on the psychosocial effects of vitiligo, Porter et al. (1986) compared vitiligo patients with a matched sample of control subjects with no skin disease, a matched sample of psoriasis patients and a matched sample of patients with other pigmentary disorders involv-

Table 2.1 Skin disorders thought to be psychogenic

Dermatitis artefacta:	The patient usually presents with lesions in accessible sites. These tend to have oddly linear or angular shapes which do not conform to natural disease. Blisters or bruises are also sometimes present. This condition tends to occur more commonly in women.
Delusions of parasitosis:	Patients with this condition believe that their skin is infested with parasites. They often present with scarred hypopigmented lesions on their arms where they have attempted to remove 'the parasites'. This condition is most often seen in female patients over the age of 40. No organic psychiatric cause is thought to be associated with the condition; however comorbidity with obsessive compulsive disorder is often identified.
Trichotillomania:	Patients with this condition rub, twist and pull out their scalp or body hair resulting in the thinning of scalp or body hair (such as eyebrows or eyelashes). The condition is common in children, but is also seen in adults. It usually recovers spontaneously in children, but the prognosis is not as good in adults if left untreated. Treatment for anxiety is often effective for the symptoms.
Neurotic excoriations:	The forearms, back of the neck and other accessible parts of the skin are most commonly involved in this condition. Excoriated lesions ranging from ulcers to healed scars are present. The lesions result from an uncontrollable urge to scratch, even though there is no primary lesion to account for this.

ing discoloration. Their results suggested that vitiligo patients exhibited better adjustment to their disorder than did psoriasis patients. However, they scored lower than the 'normal' control group in terms of self-esteem. Vitiligo patients did not differ significantly from those patients with other pigmentary disorders. A possible reason for the difference in adjustment between psoriasis and vitiligo patients may be that whereas vitiligo patients had to come to terms with the fact that the appearance of their skin changed due to formation of depigmented patches, the texture and sensitivity of their skin was unaffected. In the case of psoriasis sufferers however, the additional burden of having to cope with dry, flaking skin may compound psychological problems. The fact that both the vitiligo and psoriasis patient groups did not differ on scores on the self-esteem scale, but scored lower than the control group, suggests that self-esteem may be related more to the cosmetic consequences of a skin condition than to the practical needs and sensory changes of the condition.

Erroneous and negative beliefs about skin disease directly affect how people cope with, react to or treat their condition. Boxes 2.7 to 2.12 outline some commonly held misconceptions about common skin conditions.

Box 2.7 Myths about acne

Acne is related to diet – no evidence exists to suggest that any particular foods are directly implicated in the pathophysiology of acne.

Acne results from a person's inability to properly 'take care of themselves' – acne is actually due to inherited factors that are implicated in increased sebum production, and has nothing to do with how well a person 'takes care of themselves'.

Strong cleansers and constant scrubbing are helpful – this can actually lead to increased inflammation; mild non-abrasive cleansing is most helpful.

Acne is just a stage that people go through during adolescence – acne may actually begin in or persist through adult life and can affect a person's self-esteem whatever the age of onset (Bondi et al., 1991).

Box 2.8 Myths about eczema

Frequent bathing of the affected areas is helpful and soothing – frequent bathing and long hot showers should be avoided, moisturising preparations instead of soaps should be used and moisturisers also applied liberally after bathing may be helpful.

Eczema is contagious – eczema is not contagious, and one cannot acquire the condition by coming into contact with an eczema sufferer or his/her belongings.

Only children get eczema – although it is common in children, the condition is often seen later in life. Lesions in adults may appear at different sites however.

Box 2.9 Myths about vitiligo

Vitiligo is closely connected to leprosy – vitiligo has long been associated with leprosy due to the fact that the latter condition may also appear as hypopigmented lesions which can resemble vitiligo. However the two are not in any way connected. Leprosy is caused by a bacterium called *mycrobacterium laprae* and is contagious; vitiligo is genetically determined, immunologically based and not contagious.

Vitiligo is a problem only for people with highly pigmented skins – the idea that the more obvious that a condition is the more problems it will cause is not necessarily true. Various factors affect the extent to which patients are affected by their condition, and culture and social support have been found to be more significant than skin colour.

Vitiligo is related to the consumption of certain foods – a common belief is that eating two white food products simultaneously (i.e. milk and eggs) will cause or exacerbate vitiligo. However, there is no empirical or theoretical evidence whatsoever to support this belief, white food products not having been shown to contain any substances that will depigment the skin.

Box 2.10 Myths about psoriasis

Psoriasis is contagious – as is the case with many visible skin conditions, psoriasis is thought by some lay people to be contagious. This is not the case however and no amount of physical contact with a sufferer or his/her belongings can transmit the condition.

The discomfort caused by psoriasis is minimal; 'it's just dry skin' – the severity of this condition can vary greatly between individuals. Thus whereas some people experience little disruption to their lives and only minor physical discomfort, others are affected by more severe forms of the condition. Psoriatic arthritis may also affect approximately 5% of psoriasis patients and cause painful swelling of the joints similar to that of rheumatoid disease. This has serious consequences for patients and can significantly affect physical functioning

Box 2.11 *Myths about strawberry naevi and port-wine stains*

Strawberry birthmarks are caused by mothers eating strawberries while pregnant – as is the case with many other visible skin diseases, food is again often thought to be implicated in their etiology. This is particularly true of strawberry or port-wine stains which often have a distinctive shape and colour. In some parts of the world folklore dictates that a pregnant woman's every craving needs to be satisfied or the child will be born with a mark signifying the unsatisfied craving. In other parts of the world the opposite is true and mothers who eat too much of a particular food are thought to be responsible for the shape and colour of their child's birthmark. There is not the remotest evidence to suggest, however, that these beliefs are valid.

The shape of a mark has a particular significance – this belief centres around the view that the shape of a lesion has a mysterious or prophetic quality. This conception may have its original foundations in biblical teachings where having a mark, for example the number 666, prophesies something evil about the bearer of that mark. Similarly it is often said that a mark shaped like a horseshoe indicates that the person bearing it will be lucky. There is of course no evidence to suggest that this is true.

Box 2.12 *Myths about malignant melanoma*

This only affects people who live in very hot sunny countries – this is untrue. Indeed the harmful rays of the sun may be more dangerous to sun worshippers from cool climates who then expose their skin to the sun intensively over short periods, rather than those who expose themselves steadily and moderately throughout the year (Bondi et al., 1991).

If I am naturally dark skinned then I am not likely to get melanoma and don't need protection in the sun – although people with darker skins are less likely to become sun damaged this by no means makes them 'immune' to melanoma. It is therefore important that no matter what colour the skin is, reasonable precautions be taken in the sun

Conclusion

This chapter has highlighted how the typology of skin problems can influence people's adaptation to their condition. Factors such as the way the condition was acquired, the course it will take and the physical and sensory changes that accompany it will all play a part in the way that patients adapt to and comes to terms with their skin problem. In many cases, patients' beliefs about the course, cause and cure of their illness can have a negative impact on their adjustment. Indeed these perceptions are frequently based on myths and erroneous lay views that may need to be dispelled by health professionals (see Chapter 9). It is important therefore that we have an understanding of our patients' illness experiences and take into account how factors such as those described above can influence their adjustment and coping.

3

Coping and Adaptation

Introduction

In the preceding chapter we focused on the typology of skin conditions and the way that this can affect adjustment. The present chapter builds on this by elaborating further on factors which affect the adaptation and coping process. Personality traits, the severity of a condition and the length of time a person has lived with the illness are all considered with regard to the adaptation process. We also discuss the various behavioural and affective changes that may accompany the onset of a skin condition and the adaptation tasks that people engage in to cope with these.

Stages of adjustment

Irrespective of whether a dermatological condition is acquired congenitally or later on in life, there is a period of psychological adjustment that patients must go through in order to come to terms with their appearance. In the case of a traumatic disfigurement or the onset of a skin disease in adulthood, the person goes through a period of mourning for his or her 'normal' appearance (Partridge, 1994). As they adjust, they may experience feelings of shock, denial, anger and sadness, before coming to terms with their 'new' face or body. Mourning for the loss of 'normality' may also be experienced in the case of congenital disfigurement. The person may be preoccupied with feelings of loss associated with an image of the person they could have been (Bradbury, 1996). There may be wide variations in how people cope with, and adapt to, the impact of skin disease. These variations are not simply a product of the severity of the condition, but rather they are the result of an interaction of factors including social support, social skills, optimism, perceptions of self-efficacy and coping style (Lazarus, 1993; Kleber and Brom, 1992). Some people may find the support of friends and family sufficient to help them cope with the challenges of skin disease, while others may require the intervention of professionals to help them cope.

Specific personality traits in people with dermatological problems have also been studied. Researchers have examined the extent to which anger was implicated in the onset and maintenance of atopic dermatitis, and whether patients felt that they could cope with and manage their anger better than psoriasis patients and matched controls (Ginsburg et al., 1993). The results indicated that patients with atopic dermatitis became angry more easily, as indicated by the Siegel Multidimensional Anger Inventory, but were less inclined to display their anger than were matched controls. The patients in this group were also found to be more anxious and less assertive than the controls. However, since the study employed a cross-sectional design, it could not be determined whether these personality traits and coping styles were present before the onset of the illness or whether they were the result of coping with the illness. The efficacy of psychological interventions designed to help subjects manage their anger was not examined in the study.

Others have considered the impact of psychological interventions and how these affect the progression of various cutaneous conditions (e.g. Cole et al., 1988; Horne et al., 1989). The impact of group therapy involving relaxation techniques and behavioural interventions on patients suffering from eczema has been studied (Cole et al., 1988). Ten adult subjects received group therapy as a supplement to their regular medical regime. Symptoms were examined bi-weekly and rated in order to establish a baseline and to measure treatment effects. Patients showed significant improvement in targeted symptoms. However, it was not clear whether or not the changes in the patients' condition could be attributed to the group therapy they received. As the authors themselves point out, the small sample size, absence of independent raters to examine patients and the increased time spent with doctors need to be taken into account when interpreting and drawing conclusions from the results. Below, we discuss how people try to cope with skin problems.

Coping with the disfiguring effects of skin disease

Some patients complain that health care professionals are sometimes unhelpful or dismissive. They are told: 'It's only a cosmetic disorder,' or: 'It has no debilitating effects'. Unfortunately these utterances capture neither the severity nor the complexity of the sufferer's experience. More importantly, they minimize the distress and feelings of self-consciousness experienced by many patients. The disfiguring nature of certain skin conditions suggests that patients not only have to contend with the concept of themselves as 'ill', but also have to deal with an altered body image, and in some cases, disfigurement. In the field of disfigurement research, one of the most commonly asked questions of health care professionals is what types of problems people with an altered appearance experience. Not surprisingly, given the social significance of one's appearance, many of the problems identified stem from social encounters and reactions from others. The research literature suggests that people whose appearance deviates from the norm have difficulties meeting new people (Porter et al., 1990), embarking on close personal relationships and feeling positive about career goals and prospects (Beuf, 1990).

It has been found that the longer someone lives with a condition, the easier it becomes to cope with it (Malt, 1980; Patterson, 1993; Papadopoulos et al., 1998). It should be noted, however, that many studies of coping and adjustment employ a cross-sectional as opposed to a longitudinal design. Therefore it is not always possible to say whether the people actually become better adjusted over time or whether they had always been able to adjust well to illness-related issues.

The amount of social support a person can draw on, their social skills, levels of optimism and their beliefs about the illness all affect the way in which people with specific stressors cope. Evidence from research suggests there is no single mode, which accounts for why some people adjust well to the challenges of disfigurement while others do not. However, the results of research also suggest that equipping people with specific coping strategies can positively affect their ability to deal with their condition (see Chapter 9).

Adjusting to changes in physical appearance

In many cases, people who have become disfigured or deformed have to adapt to a new body image. They need to get used to their new appearance and learn to cope with the challenges of living with an appearance which deviates from the norm. In the case of skin disease, however, adapting to a new body image is further complicated by the fact that some skin conditions are episodic in nature. That is, the nature and severity of certain conditions fluctuates. This means that the dermatology patient may have to adapt to a changing body image. A 32–year-old female psoriasis patient describes her feelings of living with such a condition in Box 3.1

Box 3.1 Adapting to changes in appearance: a psoriasis patient's account

'Every morning the first thing that I do when I wake up is to check my body to see if the patches have changed. I know the exact shape and size of every patch and if I notice a new one then I feel almost sick to my stomach. It's so hard because you don't know what to expect. Last year I could wear short skirts, this year I can't do that anymore because the patches on my legs are so ugly, who knows what I'll have to wear next year to hide them.'

This patient's account conveys the feelings of anxiety, uncertainty and helplessness that often accompany the diagnosis of a skin condition. Without the knowledge of when or how the condition will develop, the patient may be left wondering about what behaviours or actions might be contributing to its progression. Lifestyle or diet may be affected, or in some cases particular rituals are adopted in order to gain some control over the course of their condition. Some patients who suffer from acne can, for example, expose their skin to the sun for excessive amounts of time since they believe that the sun will 'dry up' their pimples.

So far we have considered how people's adjustment to their condition may be affected by factors relating to severity, personality, cause and course. The remainder of the chapter focuses upon some of the adaptation tasks and behavioural changes which may result from living with a skin problem. The intention is to highlight common problems and issues which arise when living with a skin condition. How these problems can be addressed from a counselling perspective is discussed in detail in Chapter 8.

Living with uncertainty

Since many skin conditions occur intermittently or are progressive, patients need to address issues relating to change, loss of control and uncertainty. As is the case with many illnesses, patients may go through a period of mourning for a lost sense of normality. This may be related both to the person's appearance, if it has been altered by the condition, and also to the patient's day to day activities. Tom, a 27–year-old psoriasis sufferer, describes his feelings in Box 3.2.

> *Box 3.2 Mourning for a sense of 'normality': a case of psoriasis*
>
> 'I used to love to swim, it was something that I took up about five years ago and was practically addicted to ever since. At first when I noticed the psoriasis around my knees it didn't bother me, but since then I have begun to feel like people are avoiding me, like they look at me and know I'm different. I don't feel normal anymore, I feel that people are looking at me and wondering what happened or thinking "oh he must be so brave to be able to swim looking like that". Consequently, I have cut down on how often I go swimming and how often I'm seen in clothes that reveal the psoriasis.

Tom describes the fact that he no longer feels that others see him in the same way that they used to before he developed psoriasis. He also indicates that he no longer sees himself in the same way and that he no longer feels normal. Tom's description suggests that he feels his condition affects his self-confidence and dominates what people see when they look at him. An important task in counselling is to allow the patient to integrate living with their condition into their body image and work on accepting it as something which is a controllable part of who they are rather than as something that completely dominates their lives.

Becoming sensitized to other people's reactions

One of the biggest challenges of living with a skin disease is having to cope with the reactions of others. People may experience a variety of reactions ranging from rude comments to questions about their condition or blatant staring. These reactions can leave them feeling that their privacy has been invaded. They may feel ill-equipped to deal with the reactions of others and consequently may avoid or overreact to situations where this might be an issue. Counselling can help patients to identify practical ways of coping with such reactions. A detailed discussion of these techniques is described in Chapter 9.

Modifying appearance and behaviour to hide lesions

People with skin conditions may draw attention to themselves not because of the skin disease itself but rather because of the way they cope with and react to it. They may begin to avoid eye contact when in social situations, wear their hair so that it covers affected parts of their face, or choose to wear clothes that conceal the condition but may be inappropriate for the weather. Their reactions may give rise to a self-fulfilling prophecy. They expect that others will react unfavourably and so they seek to conceal the problem. This attempted solution may give rise to a new problem: conspicuity. These expectations, although justified in some cases are often the product of negative beliefs that patients hold about their condition. Box 3.3 outlines some of these beliefs.

Box 3.3 Negative beliefs commonly held by dermatology patients

- thinking that everybody believes that the condition has to do with a lack of hygiene or is contagious
- feeling that the first thing that people will notice about them will be the skin condition
- believing that the skin condition will prevent enjoyment of life or fulfilment of ambitions
- justifying to themselves that when things go wrong, it is due to having a skin problem
- buying into the beauty myth and the idea that all good things come to those who are beautiful

---

Structuring life around disease: 'when it gets better I will ...'

One of the most common coping mechanisms displayed by people with skin problems is a desire to treat and get rid of the condition rather than getting on with living with it. Behaviours such as taking up new sports, applying for a promotion or even getting married are postponed in the hope that the condition will be cured, enabling them to lead more enjoyable lives. Box 3.4 contains a transcript from a session with a 22–year-old Asian woman who had recently been diagnosed with vitiligo.

Box 3.4 Transcript from initial counselling session

Patient: ... my sister is married and has two kids ... that is all I ever really wanted to do with my life but I have decided, and told my parents not to try and arrange any marriages until this

---

[pointing at arms] is gone.

Counsellor: What if it takes a long time for the patches to go away or what if the white marks stay the way they are now forever?

Patient: I am sure that if a man was to see me now that he would not want me anyway, so I am going to wait until they go away and then I can think about letting my parents arrange a marriage.

Counsellor: It sounds like you are certain about the way that such a meeting would turn out. Aren't you limiting your chances of achieving your goal, to get married and have a family, by not allowing your parents to arrange these meetings?

Patient: No because I am sure ... 100% sure that no one would want me looking like this. When I am better then I can start thinking about it again.

This patient expresses the view that, as a person with vitiligo, she is undesirable and that none of her dreams or ambitions can be achieved while she has vitiligo. An attempt to challenge her thoughts exemplifies her negativity about the condition and her conviction that she cannot 'get on with her life' until she has been treated for vitiligo. One of the main focuses in counselling would be to help this patient to challenge these thoughts and gain insight into where these beliefs are coming from and which behaviours, or sociocultural influences, serve to reinforce or maintain them.

Some patients attribute negative life events to the onset of their condition and hold on to the belief that anything bad that happens in their lives must be attributed to their illness. This can lead to a cycle whereby negative life experiences serve to reinforce beliefs that the condition is ruining their life and to the feeling that there is no point in trying to change this cycle until the condition improves.

Choosing whether or not to discuss the condition

Since many dermatological conditions are immediately visible to others, patients may have no choice as to whether or not they wish to disclose the fact that they have a skin condition to those around them. Other illnesses, which are less prominent, can remain private and personal matters until the patient chooses to disclose details about them. The dermatology patient may feel that this choice has been taken away from them and may resent the fact that their condition is visible to others. Martin, a 32–year-old male with a large naevus covering the left side of his face, describes his feelings about this in Box 3.5.

Box 3.5 *Discussing the condition with other people: transcript from session with naevus patient*

'... and what really annoys me is the fact that people feel as though it's all right to come up to me and ask me about it. On some days it doesn't bother me as much but on others I feel like telling them to piss off! I mean you would never think of going up to a complete stranger and asking them if there was something wrong with their internal organs and what happened and a million other ridiculous questions. But the fact that they can see my mark makes them for whatever reason think that they have the right to invade my privacy, to put me in a difficult and awkward position just to satisfy their own petty curiosity.'

It is clear from Martin's description that his right to privacy is taken away. The insensitive reactions of others can make a person feel that they have less control in social situations and no choice about how to react. It may be useful therefore to empower patients into taking back control in such situations and equip them with skills for dealing with these, having a quick response to rude questions or coping skills for excessive staring (see Chapter 9).

Conclusion

This chapter has attempted to highlight the impact that a skin condition can have on a person's behaviour, beliefs and more generally their day-to-day life. The stages of adaptation that people go through were discussed and the way in which factors such as typology and personality can affect adjustment were outlined. The material presented in this chapter suggests that the effects of skin disease can influence everything from what clothes a person wears to major life decisions involving relationships and career, and that it is important to acknowledge this when attempting to understand the impact of skin disease on patients.

4

Psychological Factors in the Onset and Progression of Skin Problems

Introduction

This chapter examines the reciprocal relationship between the skin and the psyche. It addresses how emotions can affect the onset and progression of different conditions, and proposes a biopsychosocial model that takes into account biological, social and psychological processes in an attempt to provide a more holistic approach to care. The main issue highlighted in this chapter is that if we can understand skin disease in terms of its effects on both body and mind, then it may be possible to offer more holistic and effective care to dermatology patients and their family or carers.

The Biopsychosocial model

Until recently, skin disease was predominantly studied from a bio-medical perspective, an approach founded on the belief that physical and mental aspects of health are mostly separate. The biomedical model takes a mechanistic view of the body, conceiving illness as an agent which disrupts normal functioning, and defining health merely as the absence of disease (see Figure 4.1).

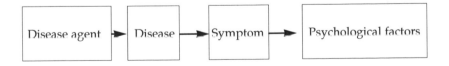

Figure 4.1 Linear view of the disease process

By emphasizing illness over health, the biomedical model focuses on anomalies that lead to illness rather than on conditions that may promote health. It is a reductionist theory, which tends to ignore the complexity of factors involved in health and illness, not recognizing the role of more general social and psychological variables.

The biomedical model has historically dominated medicine, maintaining that illness can be explained in terms of aberrant somatic processes. It assumes a mind–body dualism, maintaining that the two are independent entities (Engel, 1977). While it works well when applied to conditions resulting from specific pathogens or infectious diseases, it is of only limited use when taking into account the interplay between biological, psychological and social factors which relate to the cause, course and treatment of some skin conditions. For example, when the dry, pink lesions of psoriasis are successfully treated by a course of steroids, the cause–effect biomedical model can readily be applied to understand the change process. However, if these patches appear only when the patient suffers emotional stress, which in turn affects his sexual relationship with his partner, and which when treated with steroids responds as well as when treated with relaxation exercises, we need a more complex model to help us to understand so-called causes and effects.

In the biopsychosocial model, psoriasis is the result of a dynamic interplay between physiological processes (endocrinological imbalances), psychological states (anxiety, reduced self-esteem) and social situations (feeling embarrassed about lesions, believing that one is too unattractive to be touched). This conceptualization helps to explain the onset, maintenance and treatment effects of the problem (see Figure 4.2).

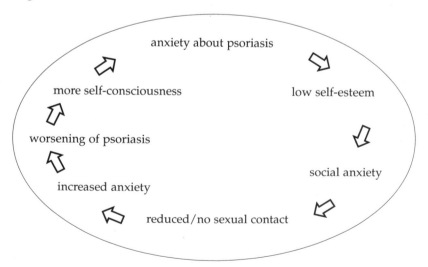

Figure 4.2: A biopsychosocial model which explains the maintenance of psoriasis

The biomedical perspective tends to ignore cognitive or behavioural factors which may cause or exacerbate a condition and consequently these are also given less attention in devising a treatment regime.

On the other hand, the biopsychosocial model of health and illness takes into account factors such as social support and psychological stress, as well as factors relating to physiological disorders or the presence of viruses. It therefore acknowledges that health and illness result from a range of factors and produce a variety of effects. Indeed, it maintains that body and mind cannot be separated in relation to health since both influence a person's health status. In cases where the illness worsens, factors such as anxiety, impaired social support, and traumatic life events have been found to be relevant. In situations where there is a stabilization or improvement in the condition, factors such as strengthened social support, improved self-esteem and enhanced self-efficacy are also thought to play a role (Kleinman, 1988). Multiple systems interact simultaneously to bring about conditions of health and illness. A system can be defined as a group of interacting or interdependent elements that form a unified whole (Von Bertallanfy, 1974). A 'systems' approach maintains that levels of organization within a system are linked and that change in any one level will effect change in others. It implies a perspective that differs from one in which biological, psychological and social factors are accounted for separately when considering illness. In the biopsychosocial approach, the system has emergent properties not predictable from the properties of the separate elements (see Figure 4.3).

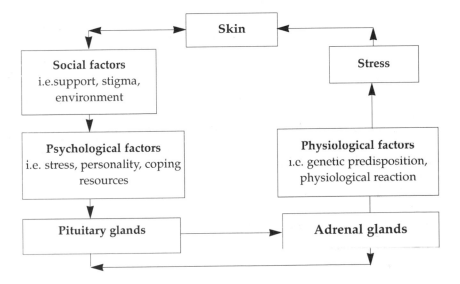

Figure 4.3. A systems perspective of the biopsychosocial model in cutaneous disease

Health, illness and health care are therefore interrelated. Health is recognized as being partly dependent on internal systems, such as the successful functioning at the cellular or organ level and partly dependent on external systems in the family and larger community. The treatment of eczema, for example, requires attention to the organ level, though many dermatologists would also agree that stress and environmental conditions may affect the course of the condition (Ginsburg and Link, 1989). Consequently, patient care requires an interdisciplinary approach to care and collaborative relationships between a range of professionals (see Chapter 12).

Effects of adjustment on the course of the condition

Individual variation exists with regard to adjustment to skin disease. While some people cope well with their condition, others become depressed and anxious about it. Interestingly, these differences are not merely a product of the severity of the condition, but rather they are the result of an interaction of variables including social support, social skills, optimism, perceptions of self-efficacy and coping style (see Chapter 6).

Although many people with skin disease cope effectively with the challenges of their condition, there exists a proportion of this population who find it difficult to cope with negative social reactions. It has been suggested that the negative reactions of people with whom dermatology patients come into contact, may predispose them to stress and anxiety, and in turn, negatively influence the physical progression of various skin conditions (Le Poole et al., 1993). This in turn may compound the psychosocial effect of the condition, thus setting up a cycle whereby skin disease negatively affects psychosocial functioning and negative psychosocial experiences affect the progression of skin disease.

In order to improve our understanding of the cause of skin disease and to treat patients effectively, there is a need to view the patient holistically, and to address the reciprocity between body and mind in relation to cutaneous disease. In other words, it is helpful to conceptualize skin disease from a biopsychosocial perspective.

Examining the 'systemic' approach to dermatology

A 'systemic' view of the dermatology patient began to emerge in the late 19th and early 20th century with the works of dermatologists such as Beard (1880), Tuke (1884), Bukley (1906) and Winkler (1911). During this period, although emotional and nervous disorders began to be cited as contributory causes of skin disease, researchers relied on anecdotal evidence of single cases to support their hypotheses. A very small number of researchers mentioned specific psychological conflicts as potential causes of these conditions. That was, apart from the growing opinion that in women anogenital pruritus had something to do with sexual pathology! Conditions of unknown aetiology tended to be associated with local 'weakness' of the nerves. The emphasis on disordered neural rather than psychological functioning clearly dominated thinking during this period.

More systematic studies on skin disease began to originate in the mid 1940s. The personality dimensions of patients with a variety of disorders were examined in relation to 'psychoneurogenous phenomena' (Stokes, 1945) – a term coined by the author. However, as was the case with much of research in this period, a lack of adequate controls in these studies meant that few meaningful data were generated from this work.

Researchers sought out specific emotional conflicts as the basis for psychosomatic conditions (Alexander, 1950; Alexander et al., 1968). Other researchers (MacAlpine, 1958) drew on this work in an endeavour to find a personality pattern for conditions such as dermatitis and alopecia areata. Attempts to identify personality traits failed however, and in more recent years this approach was abandoned in favour of methods which employ psychometric tests for examining current functioning and coping style (Finlay and Khan, 1992). Today, most researchers accept that looking for a single cause of skin disease is often not useful, and that a multifactorial approach to psychocutaneous research is needed in order to fully understand the complexities of various skin conditions.

The relationship between skin and psyche

There are several theories which postulate psychophysiological mechanisms underlying various cutaneous diseases (Whitlock, 1976; Teshima et al., 1982; Salzer and Schallreuter, 1995). In order to understand how the skin can be conceptualized from this perspective however, some general points need to be outlined.

1. Both the skin and the central nervous system develop embryologically out of the ectoderm. The central nervous system (CNS) derives from a specialized portion of the ectoderm known as the neural plate. Thus theoretically, if the two share their embryonic origin then they may be further connected in terms of their functioning.

2. Both the skin cells and certain nerve cells metabolize the amino acid tyrosine to produce either melanin or catecholamines respectively. It has been suggested that translation errors during this process may account for some of the acquired hypomelanotic disorders commonly observed (Ortonne et al., 1983; Lerner and Nordlund, 1974).

3. Apart from the dermal melanocytes, melanin-producing cells exist in other parts of the body; for example melanin is present in the brain in the substantia nigra. The fact that melanin is present in the brain prompts the suggestion that it might have biological functions other than photo-protection. Indeed, it has been shown that both naturally-occurring and drug-induced dyskinesia occurs only in species which posses melanin in the substantia nigra suggesting that melanin may have a more fundamental biological role than that of providing visible pigment.

4. There also appears to be a relationship between the skin and the immune system. Both serve the same function, but in different ways, by protecting the body from infection. Clinical studies have shown that psychological stress can cause the suppression of killer T-cells and macrophages, both of which have been shown to play important roles in skin-related immune reactions.

Each of these observations reinforces the idea that skin problems are by no means a simple physiological occurrence. Rather they are the product of an interplay between various complex systems including those of a psychosocial nature, many of which we have yet to fully understand.

Stress and skin disease: 'it doesn't affect all of the people all of the time'

Emotional factors have been linked to a wide variety of medical conditions ranging from skin disease to heart disease. This raises an interesting question: why do some people develop one form of disease in the presence of psychosocial stress while others develop something totally different, if at all? In order to understand this, it is necessary to take into account physiological systems, not only as they interact with environmental and psychological variables, but in terms of their predisposition to a particular disorder: that is, acknowledging that biopsychosocial factors interact to bring about disease not at random but rather in organs that are vulnerable or predisposed to certain conditions.

A paradigm which goes some way to explaining this is known as the diathesis stress model (Meehl, 1962). It focuses on the interaction between a predisposition towards disease (the diathesis) and environmental disturbances (stress). Although the term 'diathesis' tends to refer to a predisposition towards an illness, the term may be extended to any characteristic of the person that increases his or her chance of developing a disorder.

At a biological level, many conditions are genetically linked. Having a close relative with a disorder and sharing their genetic make-up might increase the risk for a particular disorder. On a psychological level, a person's cognitive set, the way he/she perceives the world, may predispose them to certain illnesses. For example, a chronic feeling of hopelessness may predispose an individual to developing depression.

Although possessing a diathesis for a disorder might increase a person's chances of developing it, it is not inevitable that the disorder will develop. The stress part of the paradigm accounts for how the diathesis is translated into a disorder. It indicates stressful psychological or biological environmental stimuli. Examples of this include poor nutrition, oxygen deprivation at birth or traumatic life events such as loss of employment or bereavement.

Adler's (1907) concept of organ inferiority resonates with this idea: 'Genetic factors are important determinants of the predisposition to certain diseases, for without this contribution one would have to assume that the choice of target organ was purely arbitrary' (cf. Whitlock, 1976, p. 18). Thus in the case of skin disease the skin might represent the weak organ, so that emotional and psychological disturbances are expressed through illnesses of the skin.

In their research on relaxation therapy for the treatment of psoriasis, for example, Winchell and Watts (1988) suggest that individuals inherit or acquire a basic organ inferiority that will determine the results of psychological/emotional upsets so that autonomic activity may be directed towards the weak organ. The biopsychosocial view of the dermatology patient allows one to speculate about acquired or genetic predispositions to illness, thus offering an explanation for why the same noxious external stimulus can precipitate skin disease in one person and something completely different in another. The impact of stress (as indicated by the diathesis-stress model) is a personal, subjective experience that will affect people to varying degrees depending upon their perception of how unpleasant a particular stressor is, and the coping mechanisms that they have in place to cope with it.

Although there has been an emphasis in the field of dermatology on the recognition that psychological health may affect the onset and progress of skin conditions, a detailed understanding of the links between psychological health and the onset and course of many cutaneous conditions is still not well established. It has been suggested that psychosomatic mechanisms precipitate skin disease in predisposed subjects. Others have hypothesized that people suffering from psychological problems are likely to present to their dermatologist because of hypochondriasis, delusions related to the appearance of the skin and self-mutilation. Still others have supported the view that the social stigma associated with disfiguring skin conditions might precipitate psychiatric disturbance in otherwise 'normal' subjects. There have also been suggestions that systemic diseases, such as lupus erythematosus, may produce both skin lesions and psychiatric disturbances.

Each of these ideas lends support to the application and viability of the biopsychosocial approach and a strong mind–body connection in dermatology.

The connection between the two appears to have several functions.

1. The skin not only plays an important role in tactile reception, but also responds perceptibly to emotional stimuli. Therefore skin disease may also affect tactile communication, sexual interaction and social relationships.
2. Another important link between the dermis and psychosomatics is that skin disease may signal internal pathogenic processes. For example, the diagnosis of meningococcal meningitis is often made by looking for the petechial or purpuric rash which erupts on the skin.
3. Anxiety and blushing also manifest in the form of changes in the colour or texture of the skin. The skin is metaphorically a door to physical and psychological problems and processes.

Examining the link between mind and body

The skin is a complex system made up of glands, blood vessels, nerves and muscle elements, many of which are controlled by the autonomic nervous system, and can be influenced by psychological stimuli. These have the capacity to cause autonomic arousal and the capability of affecting the skin and the development or treatment of various skin disorders. Evidence of the strong relationship between the central nervous system (CNS) and the skin has been demonstrated through stimulation of the CNS which will often produce blushing, pallor and perspiration. These psychosomatic factors can have an impact on the onset and prognosis of many skin conditions.

In their attempt to demonstrate the close relationship between the skin and the CNS, Bethune and Kidd (1961) demonstrated how they could initiate CNS (including autonomic nervous system) activity through hypnosis. They suggested that if physiological changes could be induced in the laboratory through psychological stimuli, then common everyday experiences could also produce such responses through similar mechanisms. It is these mechanisms that the authors suggested were responsible for psychosomatic effects on organ systems. It has been suggested that people may inherit or acquire a predisposition to a particular cutaneous disease and that this will determine the way in which a person is affected by the psychosomatic effects of autonomic arousal. Thus, if one's anxiety response and auto-nomic response in the skin, for example, is heightened, the resulting increase in autonomic activity may have a negative effect on the func-tioning of the skin. Other researchers (Winchell and Watts, 1988) have upheld this theory using psoriasis as an example. They suggested that in the case of psoriasis patients the skin may represent the weak organ and that increased stress may have an impact on the production of psoriatic lesions by changing autonomic activity. If the person becomes stressed or anxious about the disorder then this may result in further over-activity in the skin, producing an anxiety response habit.

The psychophysiological mechanisms of other cutaneous condi tions have also been demonstrated. In the cases of urticaria and eczema, suggestions of a psychosocial basis of the illnesses date back to the work of Wilson (1863) and Hillier (1865), who concluded that mental excitement, nervous debility and anxiety were a cause of these conditions. More recently, it has been suggested that emotional factors probably produce the effects of the illness by causing an increase in vasodilatation under the influence of histamine release in the skin (Teshima et al., 1986). As is the case with other skin conditions that are thought to have a psychological basis, urticaria has been found to respond favourably to hypnotic suggestion. An investigation was undertaken among vitiligo sufferers to examine the possibility of impaired catecholamine metabolism in vitiligo patients (Salzer and Schallreuter, 1995). The study examined whether patients displayed increased stress sensitivity to environmental or hormonal changes in relation to a defective catecholamine metabolism. The results indi-cated that norepinephrine levels in plasma were significantly higher than in controls. Although no specific personality structure was found, divergencies from the normal control were observed in five out of the twelve personality dimensions measured. The results of the study suggested a possible link between catecholamine-based stress and the progression of vitiligo.

As already mentioned, many studies which have examined the psy-chophysiology of cutaneous illnesses have considered the immune system as a contributing mechanism. This is probably due to the common function that the skin and the immune system serve. Both the skin and the immune system serve as protection against foreign organ-isms. While the immune system fights foreign bodies on the inside, the skin works to protect against invasion from the outside. This occurs on an interdependent basis, and a function of the immune system is to maintain a homeostasis of the body thereby limiting the stress inflicted upon it. In a study which examined the psychosomatic aspects of skin disease in relation to immunology, Teshima et al., (1982) found that emotional stress had the capacity to influence the immune system to a considerable degree, and this would often manifest in cutaneous illness. They found that tension in patients could lead to an enhancement of allergic reactions, and that allergic patients improved with autogenic training and relaxation.

Certain immune responses are visible on the skin, as in the cases of allergic rashes to medication or foods, and certain drug reactions. Interestingly, several psychogenic drugs which have been used to treat dermatology patients have been found to produce allergic reactions. Skin eruptions caused by barbiturates, hypnotics and non-barbiturate sedatives are common, especially in cases of overdose. The question regarding the influence of emotional states on allergic mechanisms, however, remains unresolved. There is evidence to suggest that psychological factors can influence the immune system and that hypnosis and the emotional state of the patient may alter allergic reactions.

Methods for assessing the role of psychological factors in the onset and progression of skin disease

The discussion so far suggests that some skin problems are caused, triggered or exacerbated by a range of difficulties including emotional stress, allergic reactions, illness or behavioural patterns such as lack of sleep. Some practitioners working in the fields of psychology and dermatology have attempted to examine the efficacy of different therapeutic models and techniques. One of the most common methods for doing this is through the use of validated questionnaires. These can be used to assess differences both between and within groups for research and also provide useful assessment tools for gauging the psychosocial impact that a particular condition has on a patient. Appendix 1 has a list of validated questionnaires specifically designed for use with dermatology patients, and we are grateful to the authors for permission to reprint them.

In a retrospective study which examined the relationship between stress and the exacerbation of skin conditions it was found that stress was likely to be associated with the onset of a range of skin disorders (Al'Abadie et al.,1994). Stressful life events identified by patients included family upsets such as bereavement, work and difficulties at school. They suggest that psychological interventions may be helpful for particular patients. In another study, researchers interviewing patients attending a dermatology clinic asked about the occurrence of any emotional upsets just prior to the onset of their skin condition (Greismar, 1978). Patients identified numerous stressors for a range of dermatological problems, suggesting a link between stress and skin disease, though not necessarily a causal one.

Trends in psychocutaneous research

The methods used over the past three decades to examine links between the psyche and the dermis have varied (see Table 4.1). Early research in this field often took the form of single case studies with few attempts to evaluate the progress of patients after the termination of therapy, or to compare results with those of other patients or matched controls. Outcome measures of these earlier studies were sometimes crude and usually involved the undocumented observations of a single clinician. Furthermore, outcome was often measured by changes to either psychological or dermatological variables, but rarely to both. Since the early 1980s, psychocutaneous research has begun to examine outcome from both perspectives, with the majority of research taking the form of controlled trials with large samples and quantitative, cross-sectional designs. Currently, the majority of research in this field comes from western countries and therefore results relating to variables such as coping and stigma may be culturally determined and cannot readily be generalized to other populations (see Table 4.1).

Some studies, which have examined psychological factors relating to the onset of cutaneous conditions have relied on the retrospective and subjective accounts of patients. Few studies have been conducted longitudinally to establish the links between psychology and biomedical processes. Much of the research on stress and the relationship this has with skin disease has focused on objective measures of stressful life events rather than using subjective measures of coping with stress which may be appropriate for use in this context. Furthermore, since the majority of studies have tended to be quantitative in design, much of the depth of information regarding a patient's beliefs about skin disease is invariably lost. Finally, most psychocutaneous research has been conducted on adult samples and only limited information exists in this field on children and adolescents.

Conclusion

Although we have come a long way in our understanding of the relationship between psychosocial factors and skin disease there is still a need for more research to fill in certain gaps in existing knowledge. A greater understanding of the effectiveness of enhancing patients' coping strategies through psychological counselling is needed. There is a move in medicine generally and in dermatology in particular towards gaining a holistic understanding of the individual rather than maintaining the focus on either mind or body. The recognition that cognition, emotion, motives and behaviour have an impact on skin

Table 4.1. Selected Studies in the Field of Psychocutaneous Research (1961–1997)

research topic	N	condition(s)	measures
effects of group therapy in reducing target symptoms related to skin disease	10	eczema	dermatological assessment
feelings of stigmatization in skin disease	100	psoriasis	stigma questionnaire devised for purposes of study; demographic data
effects of psychotropic medication on psychocutaneous illness	70	unspecified psychocuta- neous + anxiety and depression	Hamilton rating scales for anxiety and depression; clinical global impression; cutaneous symptoms (assessed by dermatologist & patients)
autonomic reactivity in dermatology patients	24	psoriasis	heart rate, blood pressure, orthostatic test, Valsava's manoeuvre, Stroop test, numerical square test
racial variation to physical stigma	158	vitiligo	questionnaire devised for the purpose of the study
impact of emotional factors on skin disease	94	atopic dermatitis	Spielberg Anxiety Inventory; Siegel Multidimensional Anger Inventory; Gambrill–Richey Assertion Inventory; Beck Depression Inventory; Levenson
effect of skin disease on psychological distress	22	psoriasis	Psoriasis Disability Index; General Health Questionnaire; dermatological assessment

type of study	location	Reference
cross-sectional control	USA	Cole et al. (1988)
descriptive survey	USA	Ginsburg and Link (1989)
cross-sectional double blind randomized	Belgium	Heindrickz et al. (1991)
cross-sectional control	Prague	Pankova (1991)
cross-sectional comparative analysis	USA	Porter and Beuf (1994)
cross-sectional control	USA	Ginsburg et al. (1993)
cross-sectional correlational analysis	UK	Root et al. (1994)

Table 4.1. (cont) Selected Studies in the Field of Psychocutaneous Research (1961–1997)

research topic	N	condition(s)	measures
effect of stress and the onset and progression of skin disease	329	psoriasis, urticaria, eczema, acne, alopecia, naevi, malignant melanoma, basal cell carcinoma	open-ended questionnaire
stress as a trigger for skin disease	1000	vitiligo	structured interview
perceived stigma in skin disease	614	vitiligo	Rosenberg Self-esteem Scale; General Health Questionnaire; Dermatology Life Quality Index; adapted version of Ginsburg and Links (1989) stigma questionnaire; a self-report measure of vitiligo coverage
psychiatric illness in patients referred to a dermatology–psychiatry clinic	149	eczema, psoriasis, alopecia areata, acne, dermatological non-disease, scratching without dermatological cause, dermatitis artefacta, delusional hypocondriasis	clinical psychiatric evaluation; ICD 10 classification of mental and behavioural disorders; dermatological assessment

type of study	location	Reference
retrospective qualitative analysis	UK	Al'Abadie et al. (1994)
cross-sectional descriptive analysis	India	Behl and Kappor. (1995)
cross-sectional descriptive analysis	UK	Kent and Al'abadie. (1996)
cross-sectional descriptive analysis	UK	Woodruff et al., (1997)

disease (and perhaps vice versa) opens up new possibilities regarding assessment and treatment, and the potential for exciting initiatives in the field of psychodermatology.

A systemic model of skin disease enables us to go further than simply acknowledging that multiple systems interact to produce states of health and illness by providing evidence for the reciprocity between body and mind. In order to understand the psychological consequences of cutaneous illness and to treat these effectively, there is a need to view the patient holistically, and to address the reciprocity between body and mind. Medical interventions for dermatology patients have received the most attention in the published literature and are the primary form of treatment for sufferers. The remainder of this book considers the place of psychological counselling as an adjunct to this.

5

Psychological Impact on Body Image, Self-esteem and Quality of Life

Introduction

Box 5.1. 24 year-old-acne sufferer

'I was 16 when I developed acne. Up until then I had always considered myself quite pretty. People had even asked me if I'd ever considered doing any modelling. It makes me really sad to think about that stuff now. I could have been so much more, I could have done so much more. But all I am is an unattractive, boring person who never has and never will achieve anything. You see, it's hard to feel good about yourself when you hate the person who looks back at you from the mirror every morning.'

This quotation is taken from a counselling session with a young woman who developed severe acne on her face and back during adolescence. Her words capture the profound psychological effect that a skin condition can have on body image and self-esteem. Her reference to *who she could have been* suggests that people tailor their aspirations and goals to their perception of who they are. **Body image** is an important part of this self-perception, and is closely linked with both self-esteem and quality of life. This chapter addresses in more detail the personal experience of the dermatology patient and methods of coping. The focus is on the way that people internalize the effects of their condition and integrate these into the view they have of themselves. By examining how skin conditions can affect self-esteem, body image and quality of life, it is hoped that the reader will gain further insight into the specific issues which face dermatology patients and set the groundwork for the chapters which follow on working psychotherapeutically with this patient group

Psychological effects of skin conditions

Skin conditions can give rise to a range of psychological problems in affected individuals. These include low self-esteem, social anxiety, altered **self-concept** and depression (Kent et al., 1995; Lansdown et al., 1997). In a study which sought to examine how peoples' lives are affected by the onset of different skin conditions, researchers interviewed 100 people with acne, psoriasis or eczema who attended a hospital outpatient clinic (Jowett and Ryan, 1985). They found that patients' lives had been affected in several ways by their skin condition, including lowered self-esteem and difficulties in relationships, as well as reduced opportunities in finding employment, functional and interpersonal problems in the workplace, increased levels of anxiety, lack of self-confidence and depression. Eighty per cent of patients indicated that they were embarrassed and self-conscious about their appearance and felt that people were likely to stare at them. However other clinicians have found that people who have suffered burns, have port-wine stains or other disfiguring skin conditions cope well with their appearance and in some cases do not differ at all in terms of psychological adjustment when compared to non-disfigured people (Blakeney et al., 1988).

Clinicians have debated what it is that allows one person to adapt to, and cope well with, their condition while others become reclusive. One explanation might be that the severity of the skin condition is a good predictor of adjustment: that is to assume that patients who have more obvious or severe skin diseases are affected to a greater extent than those whose conditions are less serious. Others have suggested that the prominence of the condition may be a factor in adjustment (Williams and Griffiths, 1991; Hughes et al., 1983). However this observation is not well supported when subjected to scientific study (Baker, 1992; Malt and Ugland, 1989). One might expect for example that darker skinned vitiligo patients would suffer more than lighter skinned patients since the condition is more conspicuous on darker skins. However, in a recent study of psychological reactions to vitiligo between different races, it was found that Afro-Caribbean respondents were not significantly more depressed than Caucasian respondents. Asian members of the sample were found to be significantly more negative about the consequences of their condition than either black or white respondents, possibly suggesting that a more culturally bound explanation for this negative self-image is more likely (Papadopoulos et al., 1998).

It has been suggested that gender is a factor which mediates the psychological consequences of disfiguring skin conditions, with women being more negatively affected by their condition than are men. This belief stems from research which suggests that women spend more money on improving their physical attractiveness (Kleinman, 1988) and experience more psychological illness thought to be related to **body image** such as anorexia nervosa and bulimia than men (Cash, 1990). Gender differences exist in terms of the social norms to which some women may feel that they are expected to conform. A woman's self-worth may be linked to her perception of how she looks and how others perceive her, whereas a man's self-worth may be more dependent on attributes such as physical fitness (Lerner and Nordland, 1974). One might expect that women are more distressed and have more adjustment problems to an altered appearance than men. Again, this is not upheld by research findings in the field. A recent example of this is a study by Brown and his colleagues (1988) which found no gender differences in the psychological adjustment of male and female burns victims. However, they noted that the methods employed for adjustment varied between the sexes. The main predictors for male adjustment were low functional disability, low use of avoidance coping and being involved in recreational activities, and for females problem solving, low functional disability and family support. It appears, therefore, that differences may lie not in psychological adjustment to disfigurement but rather in the coping methods used to aid adjustment (Robinson, 1997).

Studies such as these highlight the fact that people are not always well prepared to cope with the emotional and psychological challenges that can be brought on by a skin problem, and that a variety of complex factors can influence the extent to which a person is affected by their condition.

Body image

It has been argued that **body image** is closely related to self-concept, the development of which may be influenced by how positively or negatively we think others appraise us, 'the looking glass self' (Cash, 1986). It may be further influenced by the demands placed on the individual by their social and cultural environment. Subjective evaluations of how well a person's appearance conforms to these demands can significantly affect self-esteem and body image. Skin disease may not have to be severe for the individual to negatively evaluate their ability to conform to social standards. These social demands can be physical such as being able to play water sports in the sun without fear of exposing eczema patches or prevailing cultural beliefs and attitudes such as the belief that a tan in the summer looks attractive and healthy, and that pale or imperfect skin is unattractive.

To a large extent, body image is affected by the way we believe others perceive us. Some people choose to focus on the 'unattractive' aspects of their appearance and their body image is based on those features with which they are unhappy. It is often the case that people who are unhappy with their appearance tend to see their bodies only as aesthetic objects and minimize the functional utility of their body (see Box 5.2).

Box 5.2 *Focusing on unattractive aspects of appearance*

'I don't see what the point of working out in the gym is any more. Before the psoriasis, I looked half-decent, I had nice legs and my body was pretty toned. Since I got this, I feel unattractive no matter what I do. I mean, even if I had perfect legs or a six-pack stomach, who cares? I'd still have all this horrible flaky skin to deal with. It's like it cancels out everything else... it doesn't matter how hard you work at it, it never gets completely better, people will always notice it. I've decided that there's no point in working out any more. You see I'll never be "Pete with the nice legs", I'll always be "Pete with the horrible skin".'

People with a negative body image may develop perceptions about themselves which may dictate the behaviours or activities that they engage in and the beliefs that they have about other people's reactions towards them. The account described above also suggests that some people tend to focus only on the negative aspects of their appearance, ignoring any positive aspects. The patient above felt that psoriasis was his most salient feature, and that, regardless of whether or not other aspects of his appearance were attractive, people would not be able to see past his skin problem.

A problem that further compounds the way that people with negative body image feel about themselves is the fact that some people 'edit' social and interpersonal experiences to reinforce the view of them as unattractive. For example, a person who has an exaggerated or negative view of their acne might assume that if somone asks them out on a date, it is because they feel sorry for them and not because they find them interesting or attractive. Some clinicians have suggested that the effects of stigmatization may alter an individual's cognitive processing leading them to perceive even benign responses as hostile, and to internalize these so that they lower self-esteem and perceived body image (see box 5.3) (Cash and Pruzinsky, 1990).

Box 5.3 James's diagnosis of Kaposi's sarcoma

James first developed Kaposi's sarcoma (KS) on his right eyelid 6 months after finding out that he had AIDS. Since he had lived with HIV infection for several years, he felt that he had come to terms with his illness and had coped well with the reactions of his friends and family to his condition. However, when KS appeared on his face, he became concerned about his appearance and began to feel bad in himself and worried about how people would accept him. When he went out with friends, he tried to see whether they were looking at his eyelid and would become angry if they mentioned anything relating to his condition.

The emotional impact felt by people who live with skin disease can lead to a 'social death' (McGregor, 1951) or a withdrawal from social roles. This 'social death' can affect the activities or behaviours in which a person engages, diminish the amount of social support that the person receives, and in turn affect the coping resources that they have to help them deal with their condition. This pressure has the capacity to affect not only personal and social activities, such as relationships and hobbies, but also quality of life related goals and expectations. It has been found that facially disfigured individuals with a skin disease have lower career aspirations and more negative expectations about finding a life partner than those who are not affected by a skin problem.

People with low body image are more likely to:

- edit social experiences so as to reinforce existing negative perceptions of themselves
- view their bodies only as aesthetic objects
- minimize other positive aspects of their appearance
- have a heightened sense of body awareness
- comply with narrow social standards in terms of what is attractive.

These factors can in turn lead to lowered self-esteem and reduced quality of life, which we will now discuss.

Self-esteem

Having examined the concept of body image, we now turn to a related concept, that of self-esteem. In the field of health psychology, self-esteem is considered a personal resource and it has been found to moderate the effects of disfiguring conditions, incapacitating illness, injury or threatening life events. In the field of counselling psychology, it is seen as a dynamic personality dimension that is affected by a person's interpretation of their world, the extent to which their 'real self' measures up to their 'ideal self' (Rogers, 1961) and the way they believe themselves to be perceived by others.

Self-esteem is closely associated with body image. Dissatisfaction with a particular aspect of one's self has been found to cause an overall reduction in self-esteem. The failure to live up to an ideal image in an area which is considered important to someone's self-definition can be significantly damaging to a person's self-image. The relevance of self-esteem to dermatology is that it is associated with body image, which is disturbed first with the onset of a disfiguring condition. Self-esteem is also relevant in how patients cope with their condition. It has been found that people who have positive self-esteem are better able to cope with both the reactions of others to their appearance and their own feelings about their altered appearance (Cash and Pruzinsky, 1990).

From a cognitive perspective, if a person has developed a strong positive self-concept, then negative or ambiguous social reactions will be less likely to be internalized, and in turn the psychological effects of these will be less negative (Lanigan and Cotteril, 1989). For example, staring is often a difficult problem to contend with when living with a visible skin condition. If a person has low self-esteem then this can be particularly difficult. A person is more likely to internalize the effects of staring, believing that they are unattractive and that others are repulsed by their appearance. On the other hand, if the person has high self-esteem, then they are less likely to internalize the reactions of others and make sense of the staring in terms of the other person's bad manners or curiosity.

Those who are able to maintain a high sense of self-esteem achieve this through:

- not internalizing the negative reactions of others
- being confident about their ability to cope with negative social reactions
- not relying heavily on external social standards of beauty
- believing that the negative reactions of others say more about the people exhibiting them than they do about themselves.

Quality of life

Box 5.4 26–year-old acne sufferer

'Ever since the acne has got worse, I've stopped going out with friends. I've stopped buying clothes and I've even stopped thinking about getting the promotion at work. It's like your life is on 'hold' when your skin looks like this. You don't want to do anything, you don't want to go anywhere, and the only thing that you can think about is the way you look. When I think back there are so many things that I missed out on because of my skin. I didn't go to my school dance, I never went on holidays or camping with my friends, I even didn't go to have my graduation photo taken at university, because of the acne. People think that acne is just a small problem and that it doesn't really affect your life... but for me it is my life. If I'm happy or sad, if I decide to go out or stay in, it all depends on how my skin is. It affects every part of my life, every minute of the day.'

This person's description highlights how skin disease can affect a person's quality of life. These effects can range from deciding what clothes to wear or whether to put make-up on to choices regarding relationships and career. Until recently, quality of life was defined in terms of length of survival and frequency of symptoms that an ill or handicapped person had to endure, with very little consideration given to the psychosocial consequences of the illness or the effects of treatment. Quality of life is a subjective experience which involves a series of evaluations and judgements made by the patient. The importance of the subjective nature of life quality was underscored by Jachuck and his colleagues (1982) who found that although 100% of the physicians in their study reported that their patients' quality of life had improved following treatment with medication, only half of these patients actually agreed with this. More recently, the measurement of quality of life has placed less emphasis on objective indicators of physical functioning and more emphasis on subjective psychosocial factors.

In the case of skin disease, the effects on quality of life may not be immediately obvious. Since most skin conditions tend not to be physically handicapping in any way, quality of life tends to be affected through the 'psychological handicap' that accompanies skin disease. The way that a condition affects a person's quality of life is mediated by a range of factors, both internal (self-esteem; body image) and external (social support; social stigma). Box 5.5 describes how dermatological problems can affect a person's quality of life.

Box 5.5 How skin disease can affect quality of life

- The condition may necessitate the use of medications and treatments that may be expensive and difficult and time-consuming to apply.
- Conditions that are progressive and episodic may make the person feel as though they have no control over their illness and may lead to obsessive body-checking behaviours.
- The visibility, coupled with the stigmatizing nature of some conditions, may make the person feel uncomfortable in social situations.
- The visibility of the condition may affect the person's body image and this can negatively affect social and interpersonal relationships.
- The person may go to great lengths to avoid exposure to others, taking special care over the selection of clothes, avoiding activities such as swimming and applying camouflage make-up to conceal the condition.
- Some conditions are painful and uncomfortable, and may interfere with sleep or intimate contact between the person and his or her partner.
- Some conditions require that certain foods or environments be avoided, thus limiting a person's behaviours or experiences.
- The reactions of others may be negative thus making them feel uncomfortable about engaging with others or entering into new relationships or situations.

Conclusion

This chapter has endeavoured to provide the reader with some insight into the ways that people are affected by their condition in terms of self-esteem, body image and quality of life. The importance of considering these variables was discussed in relation to how patients adjust and react to their condition. The chapter also considered how self-esteem body image and quality of life can affect, and be affected by, social and interpersonal relationships. This is explored further in Chapter 6, which examines in detail how skin disease impacts upon various relationships including those of a professional, romantic and familial nature.

6

The Impact of Skin Disease on Relationships

Introduction

The previous chapters described the emotional and psychological effects of skin disease on the individual. However, as is the case with most illnesses, skin disease has an impact on a person's relationships, which inevitably affects, and is affected by, the individual's condition. In this chapter we consider the impact that skin conditions have on different relationships and consider some of the social contexts in which difficulties regarding the skin condition may arise. The issue of social stigma is also considered. The final section of this chapter explores common difficulties that arise in social situations, such as staring and awkward questions from strangers, and ways in which people might deal with these. Although this is not intended to be a chapter on counselling, the reader will be introduced to some self-help techniques which can be taught and used in social situations. It will also set the groundwork for the second section of the book, which deals in detail with the use of counselling skills in dermatology settings.

Skin disease and relationships

Researchers have also sought to examine the impact of skin disease on patients' relationships. One study considered the social aspects of psoriasis (Dungey and Buselmeir, 1982). Because of its visibility, the condition evokes a range of responses in those who come into contact with people with the condition. Psoriasis is sometimes considered dirty, ugly or even contagious both by non-affected people and by those suffering from the condition. This has implications for both personal and intimate relationships, with patients reporting that they may avoid social contact especially where the possibility of intimacy may arise.

In an examination of the effect of vitiligo on sexual relationships, 158 vitiligo sufferers between the ages of 16 and 79 were administered a questionnaire on their beliefs regarding intimate relationships (Porter et al., 1990). One quarter of those surveyed indicated that they believed that their skin condition had adversely affected their sexual relationships. Between 10 and 15% of those surveyed indicated that their skin condition had limited their ability to find a partner, stating that the number, frequency and location where sexual relationships might occur was also limited. Contrary to what one might expect, the findings of the study suggested that the majority of patients felt more embarrassed in non-sexual interpersonal relationships than in intimate sexual and social relationships. A possible explanation for this may be that since more than half of the sample interviewed were married, with a median age of 38 years, it was likely that they had been involved in long-term relationships. In these cases the issue of their disfigurement was not something new and, probably, coping mechanisms had already been established. The possibility of a new sexual encounter was less likely than that of a social non-sexual one. It is reasonable to assume that anxiety would tend to be associated more with the latter situation. The authors of the study suggest that psychological counselling could be beneficial if it addressed self-esteem and body image.

Skin conditions can affect relationships in several ways The increased reassurance needed by patients to feel that they are still wanted by their partners may put a strain on the relationship or make the 'well' partner feel that they are insensitive and in turn out-of-touch with their partner's needs. Family rituals and routines may need to change due to illness. For example, if the patient needs to avoid the sun, summer holidays may have to be abandoned. This may result in feelings of guilt and cause resentment on the part of the partner. Social contacts, friends and acquaintances may be avoided by the patient following the onset of a skin disease. This may have the effect of decreasing the patient's social support system and place an added strain on the emotional and practical coping resources of the couple, where the patient is in a relationship.

Social stigma

Social stigma refers to the process by which a person's behaviour or appearance is considered to be deviant by others and leads to prejudicial thoughts, utterances or behaviours. Kelly, a 48–year-old mother of two with facial cancer describes her experience of stigma with a group of strangers in Box 6.1.

Box 6.1 Reactions of strangers

'I was at the cosmetics counter in a large department store when I noticed two teenage girls looking at me and laughing. They were being really rude and although I don't usually say anything … I mean I don't usually react to rude remarks, I asked them what their problem was. One of them then looked at me in disgust and said "We don't have a problem but you do because no matter how much make-up you buy you are still going to look like a freak." I was so shocked and distressed by what they had said that I ran out of the shop in tears.'

This example highlights how anonymity may lead some people to cast aside basic social norms, such as politeness and respect for others' feelings. It is common for people with visible skin conditions to be subjected to socially stigmatizing reactions from strangers rather than from people with whom they are likely to have more consistent contact. The case described above may seem extreme. However, even in cases where there is no intention to hurt or be rude, the effects of stigma are no less hurtful though rejection may be more subtle. Anthony, a 21–year-old acne sufferer, describes his experience in Box 6.2.

Box 6.2 Meeting new people

'Me and some friends, there was about five of us, we were going to a birthday party being held at the house of one of my closest friend's cousins. I had never met this cousin before but my friend said that he had told him to bring whoever he wanted to the party. When we arrived, a pretty young woman opened the door and my friend started to introduce all of us. She greeted everybody with a warm smile and a kiss on the cheek, but when it was my turn to be introduced she just smiled politely and shook my hand. I felt that I repulsed her.'

The way a person copes with these and similar situations may depend on their self-esteem and body image as well as the social skills that they have in place (see Chapter 5).

Prejudice from professional carers

Depending on the type of skin condition, patients may spend varying amounts of time with their GP, dermatologist or nurse. Consultations with professionals may also be problematic for patients depending upon the reaction of the professional towards the person. Some doctors tend to make judgements about the seriousness of a medical condition in terms of whether or not it is life threatening. Some skin conditions are consequently deemed trivial or insignificant. If this is conveyed to patients, it may leave them feeling misunderstood or embarrassed for having taken up their doctor's time. In most cases, the first professional contact for the patient with a dermatological problem is his or her general practitioner. Some patients feel that their GPs either do not take them seriously or do not or refer them to a specialist. Many dermatology patients have reported that their problem was either trivialized by their GP and they were told to 'ignore it', or were told that there was no treatment available. This can be especially upsetting if the patient has had to build up his or her confidence to talk to the doctor.

Forming new relationships

The prospect of starting new relationships is stressful for most people. The importance that is placed on first appearances in social encounters means that this can be particularly stressful for a person who suffers from a skin disease. Involvement in a new relationship raises issues for this person about body image and self-esteem and highlights insecurities about these. Indeed, since identity is to some extent linked to body image, skin disease may leave the patient feeling no longer the same person and even lead to mood or personality changes. This may in turn affect how they react and relate to those around them. Patients too bring their own beliefs and expectations to new social situations and may feel that they are expected to act in a certain way because of their appearance. Through counselling, a patient can be helped to challenge negative thoughts and find positive ways of engaging in relationships. Some of the most common issues that arise in new relationships include whether or how patients will disclose information about their condition, and how they can influence the situation to encourage others to look beyond their condition and engage with them. These ideas are discussed below.

How will others see past the skin disease?

The prominence of certain skin conditions may interfere with the normal rituals associated with encountering new social situations. Sufferers may feel as though others with whom they come in contact will be fixated by their appearance and will therefore not be able to see past their condition. This may lead to avoiding meeting new people or entering into new social or professional relationships. People who are unable to challenge their fears may withdraw from social activities, preferring to be alone rather than risk the possibility of rejection or social ridicule. The transcript in Box 6.3 is an extract from a counselling session with a 19–year-old neurofibromatosis sufferer.

Box 6.3 Excerpt of counselling session with neurofibromatosis patient

'I'm quite shy so it's really never been easy for me to go out and make friends. I guess that a big part of it is the way I look. I keep wondering what people are thinking about when they look at me... I often wonder if they feel sorry for me, if they are trying to be polite, if they are dying to ask me questions about it, but feel that they shouldn't. It is so hard to talk to someone new when you know that all the time all they can really see, or at least really focus on, is your skin! It is much easier to hang out with your family or the people you already know. At least you've been through all that stuff with them and neither of you has to feel uncomfortable...'

When do I tell them?

Depending on the location of the skin problem it may not be immediately visible and so the decision as to whether and when the person will tell others can be delayed. If, for example, the condition affects the chest or back then these may not be visible while the person is clothed. Problems may first arise in situations where they have to remove their clothing, such as when changing clothes, having sexual relations or at a public swimming pool. They have to decide at what point they want to disclose the fact that they have a skin condition to a prospective partner or new friends. Some may choose to hide the problem by making excuses to others. These may be elaborate explanations as to why they are unable to engage in activities such as tanning or having sex with their partner. Sandra, a 29–year-old eczema sufferer, describes one such situation in Box 6.4.

Box 6.4 Transcript of session with eczema patient

'I met this really cute guy at a club over Christmas and he asked for my phone number. We went out on a few dates together and things were really going well. I was very confident and didn't even think about my eczema until he asked me to spend the weekend with him. I knew we would end up sleeping together and I knew there was no way I could hide the patches. I was convinced that if he saw the way I looked that he would never want to be with me again. So I told him I couldn't go, I made up a dumb excuse about having to babysit and work. Anyway... needless to say that relationship didn't work out.'

This example illustrates how the belief that her partner would reject her because of her appearance prevented Sandra from developing a relationship with him. These convictions were based not on past experience because she had avoided other similar encounters. Rather they derived from a belief that others would not be able to accept the way she looked. A useful technique for dealing with such negative thoughts involves challenging the negative thought patterns of patients and giving them alternative frameworks within which to conceptualize their behaviour and that of others (see Chapter 9 for a detailed discussion).

The importance of disclosure may be particularly relevant in the case of HIV-associated Kaposi's sarcoma, where the condition may signal HIV infection and therefore the potential of transmission of HIV to a prospective partner. In cases such as these, the person may feel that he has no choice but to discuss his condition with others. Jonathan, a 31–year-old gay man with HIV, discusses his experience in Box 6.5.

Box 6.5 Transcript from a counselling session with a Kaposi's sarcoma patient

'When I saw the dark purple-brown mark over my nose, I knew exactly what it was and so does every other gay man that I come in contact with. KS is like a big neon light that says, "Hey look at me, I'm HIV positive!". I hate the fact that I can't choose when and how I'll tell new partners or friends about my HIV status. I hate it that my skin says so much about who I am and that I am ill. Before the KS, I felt that I could sometimes forget about having HIV. You know, just let it drift from my mind. Now all I have to do is look in the mirror or in the face of someone who has just met me and I remember ...'

Do others have a right to know?

Another issue that is important to consider is whether or not patients feel that they are ready to openly discuss their condition with others. Much of the research on coping with a visible disfigurement suggests that 'being open' and talking to others about one's illness may help to create a buffer against stress associated with health problems. However, some people may not feel that they want to tell others about their skin disease. They may feel embarrassed or value their privacy and their right to choose with whom to discuss their condition rather than satisfying what may be no more than the curiosity of a stranger. This experience of feeling that one's privacy is being invaded is captured in an extract of a counselling session with 'Sarah', a 32 year old naevus sufferer:

Box 6.6 Excerpt from session with 'Sarah', a naevus patient

'It was like the other day on the underground, this woman came up to me all smiley faced and happy, and asked me just straight like that: "What is that on your face dear? It looks painful, is it?" I mean I was reading my paper, it was after a hard day at the office and the last thing that I wanted to do was get into an in-depth discussion about my port-wine stain with a total stranger! I mean, I know that it's a good idea to try and educate people about it, but sometimes I think, well that's not my job! I mean if I had cancer or an ulcer or something internal that others couldn't see, people wouldn't expect me to answer questions about it or talk about it on the tube, would they? It's like, if they can see it, then they're allowed to ask about it. All the politeness or protocol that we have when we are around someone with an illness goes out the window. It's like our curiosity to know what "that weird looking thing" is, outweighs the importance of sparing someone else's feelings or respecting their privacy.'

Sarah's description of how it feels to have your illness 'displayed' to others suggests that there is no simple answer as to how to deal with the problem of disclosure. A range of factors have to be taken into account including the person's confidence, the nature of the encounter and relationship, the potential risks and benefits, the predicted reaction of the other person, and past experiences of disclosure, among others.

Existing relationships

Although the prospect of starting a new relationship may provoke feelings of anxiety, existing relationships can also be affected by the onset of a cutaneous illness. Insecurities may arise and people may wonder whether they will be viewed in the same way as before or be as desirable as they were prior to the onset of the condition. This will inevitably have an effect on the way that they relate to others and how they interpret others' reactions to them.

Although it is accepted that physical appearance changes with age, changes in appearance due to skin disease are not as straightforward and acceptance may not be routine. On the one hand, existing relationships may provide a source of support, buffering against distress. However, relationships may also be a source of anxiety. Some may believe, for example, that they are no longer attractive to their partner, or that work colleagues no longer respect them.

'Marissa', a 58–year-old woman with facial cancer, describes how her relationship with her husband changed following surgery where part of her nose had to be removed in Box 6.7.

Box 6.7 Excerpt from a counselling session with 'Marissa' a cancer patient

'My husband and I have been married for 30 years. He is a good man and we've always had a good marriage. But since the cancer I've been feeling that... that maybe he thinks I am ugly. Like the other night, I... well I felt like kissing him. When he said he was tired, all I heard was "you are ugly, go away". And it's hard to get those ideas out of my mind, I mean ... but for a bigger belly and less hair, he doesn't look very different to the day I married him, but me...well, I am a different person. When I tell him that I feel rejected, he says that I am being silly, but I don't believe him. I know things have changed.'

Marissa's story highlights how the 'meaning' that patients attach to events and reactions from those around them can hinder coping and delay adjustment. Her expectation that he would reject her because of the way she looked, impelled her to construe his remark as a rejection of her advances. Perhaps if Marissa and her husband had been helped to be more communicative about her condition and its effects on her appearance, her conclusion about her partner's reaction might have been different.

Having identified the problems that people with skin conditions may face and the way that situational factors can affect adjustment, we now address some common questions asked by patients when they find themselves in difficult or uncomfortable social situations.

What do I say when they ask?

The first thing to do is to decide if you want to answer the question. Remember, even though others can see it, you have the right to keep your condition private if you want to. If you do decide to discuss your condition you are in effect taking on the role of 'educator'. You might try and explain the 'cause' of your condition, how common it is and how it affects you. If you do so with some confidence, you will convey this to the other person who in turn may react more positively.

What do I do if people stare?

People stare for various reasons. They may be curious, unsettled or even being intentionally rude. In most cases however it is hard to tell which it is! Usually the best way to handle staring is to make eye contact with the person looking at you and to smile. This sends the message that you are aware that they are staring but that you are OK with the way you look and who you are. The fact that you are aware that they are staring is usually enough to make them avert their gaze. The fact that you are smiling indicates that you are confident rather than annoyed and that you are comfortable with the way you look.

Conclusion

Most medical conditions, whether they are acute or chronic, raise issues for the patient in terms of whether, when and how to tell others. Some patients with skin disease may not have this choice if their condition is visible to others. The patient becomes open to the curiosity, scrutiny or concern of those around them. The topics discussed in this chapter have centred around examining how different social relationships can be affected by skin disease. People may find themselves in a range of difficult social situations, having to contend with staring, awkward questions and remarks from curious children. Although this chapter has briefly examined possible ways that people can deal with difficult social situations, it is in the following chapters that we will consider in detail how counselling can be used to help these patients cope with the challenges of their condition.

7

Introduction to Counselling

Introduction

We turn our attention now to the use of counselling in the field of dermatology. A central theme in this chapter is the idea that people have the capacity to cope with their difficulties and to grow emotionally, given the right therapeutic climate. By engaging in a counselling or the psychotherapeutic relationship for self-exploration, people will eventually be able to articulate their difficulties and work towards their resolution. Through this process the patient is encouraged to move towards openness and self-trust as opposed to feeling either stuck or invalidated. The patient is helped to gain self-confidence rather than being subjected to what others believe he or she ought to be.

What is counselling?

The term 'counselling' is used to describe a variety of different interactions between people, and therefore we need to clarify what we mean when we use the term. In our definition, counselling is construed as an interaction in a therapeutic setting, focusing primarily on a conversation about relationships, beliefs and behaviour (including feelings), through which the patient's perceived problem is elucidated and framed or reframed in a fitting or useful way, and in which new solutions are generated and the problem takes on a new meaning.

Our definition is intentionally broad so as to take into account the fact that helping people in a therapeutic context does not necessarily imply finding solutions to their problems, but can provide a relationship where they can be helped to feel understood and better about themselves and their condition. Another important point is that the relationship between the counsellor and the patient is a collaborative one. It is not hierarchical nor is it necessarily didactic. It takes into account the fact the counsellor is viewed as a specialist in therapeutic skills, but that the patient also has expertise in the issues and problems that concern them. It is through collaboration between counsellor and patient (and other professionals) that positive outcomes in counselling are achieved.

How can counselling help in the treatment and management of dermatology patients?

Counselling can help patients to:

- come to terms with news about their condition
- explore treatment options and facilitate decision making
- discuss difficulties in relationships and how to cope with these
- examine the difficulties they are experiencing with their condition, and gain insight into what factors maintain these difficulties
- explore and challenge perceptions of poor body image and low self-esteem
- identify useful coping strategies that the patient has and enhance these
- identify existing sources of support that may facilitate coping but that are not being used
- gain insight into practical techniques that they can use to deal with awkward social situations, resulting from having to live with their condition
- examine issues that may be indirectly related to the skin condition but that compound the psychological effects of the condition.

Who provides counselling?

There is a distinction between having counselling skills and being a counsellor. Many people who work in health care, including doctors and nurses, counsel patients in the course of their work. They do this almost on a routine basis through information giving, clarifying treatment options and helping people to adjust to difficult circumstances. Specialist counsellors, on the other hand, are those people who have advanced training in counselling skills, such as psychologists, psychiatrists, psychotherapists and social workers as well as some nurses and doctors who have had professional training in counselling. In many cases, people who work medically with dermatology patients may find it difficult to adequately help patients to cope with various problems because of limitations on their time or the complex nature of these problems. In these cases, they might refer them to a specialist counsellor.

What actually happens in counselling?

There are many myths about what actually happens in counselling sessions. Some people may expect to be see a leather couch, and to be greeted by a bearded Freud-like figure asking them to talk about their mother! This is now rarely the case and modern approaches to counselling are often focused, short-term and effective. Most counsellors are concerned with helping patients to feel safe and comfortable in the counselling session so they can explore their problems with a view towards their resolution. This involves several stages including: introducing the concept of counselling to the patient; addressing any concerns that they may have about being in the session; identifying for whom the problem is most a problem, and exploring difficulties; finding out how the patient has so far attempted to solve the problem; offering suggestions for other ways to address the problem; and monitoring changes in the person, the problem and significant relationships.

In spite of advances in the modern practice of counselling, some people are still often concerned about the stigma attached to seeing a counsellor. It is therefore a good idea to first explore with the patient his or her views and expectations about counselling. Box 7.1 outlines some of the main stages of the counselling process.

Box 7.1 Stages in the counselling process

Introduction: set the context with patients: how do they feel about being there?

Listen to their issues/concerns, remember this may be the first time they have openly expressed these.

Try to clarify their problems and concerns by asking open and closed questions.

Consider the impact that their concerns are having on them and on their relationships.

Look at their beliefs about their problem.

Look at their attempted solutions.

Offer further thoughts/interventions.

Monitor and assess change.

Counselling skills

Before we can begin to help our patients through the use of counselling skills and interventions, we first need to identify and explore
their problems. A central issue that underscores many of the difficulties that patients' experience is that there may be some discrepancy
between who they perceive themselves to be and who they would like
to be. This concept of the 'real' or 'perceived' self and its relationship
to the 'ideal' self is an important theme in humanistic counselling
(Rogers, 1961). The idea behind this is that the perception that we hold
of ourselves is a combination of all the 'I' and 'we' statements that we
have heard throughout our lives. By way of contrast, our 'ideal self' is
the person that we strive to be. In cases where these two self-percep-
tions differ, emotional problems may arise. This has particular relevance to people suffering from a skin disease which may alter their
physical image of themselves and in turn may affect their perception
of who they should be. The main task of the counsellor is to help
patients examine this discrepancy and empower them to move closer
to their ideal self or help them to change their image of their ideal self.

Another important issue to consider is the fact that many of the
patients who present for counselling who have a dermatological problem may feel that others have trivialized their problem. This may have
been done with the good intent and with the goal of reassuring the
person, such as telling them that 'it's not that bad' and that 'others are
a lot worse off'. Dismissing or trivializing the problem can actually
make it far worse. For this reason, the counsellor must be attentive and
respectful and never offer false platitudes (see box 7.2).

Box 7.2 Minimizing the psychological effects of skin disease can:

- cause the patient to feel guilty about being anxious or distressed about his or her condition, or attending counselling
- make the patient feel that he or she cannot cope as well as
  others with similar conditions
- make the patient feel that they cannot or should not ask for
  support from those around them
- give rise to the belief that the feelings that they hold about
  their condition are not valid and therefore they should not
  express them but rather cope on their own.

The counselling skills outlined in this chapter are not primarily concerned with equipping the patient with practical tools and techniques
that they can use to cope with their problem, as these are described in
Chapter 9. Instead, the emphasis here is on examining the core thera-

peutic conditions that empower patients to address and cope with difficult feelings and problems that they experience. These core conditions include congruence, unconditional positive regard and empathic understanding (see Boxes 7.3 to 7.5).

Box 7.3 Congruence or genuineness

- implies that the counsellor is 'real' and authentic during the counselling session and conveys interest
- suggests that the counsellor's inner experience and non-verbal behaviour are congruent
- allows the counsellor to openly express their feelings
- leads to acceptance and the expression of feelings in the session which facilitates honest communication with the patient

---

Genuineness should not be misinterpreted as self-disclosure. A common misconception about genuineness is that the counsellor says exactly what he or she feels. This may not be helpful as the patient may feel invalidated or upstaged. However it implies that he or she is aware of what they are feeling and acts consistently with those feelings. Although its important to be honest with your patient, it is also important to keep in mind that expressing your feelings is appropriate only when it facilitates helping the patient (Martin, 1989). For example, a counsellor working with a patient who has been diagnosed with vitiligo, but who also has very pale skin so that the condition is hardly visible, may be inclined to share with their patient the idea that they can hardly see the condition. As already mentioned, although genuine, a response such as this might actually serve to trivialize the patient's experience or make them feel guilty for having talked about their condition. This is especially the case in the early stages of counselling where the therapeutic relationship has not yet been well established.

Box 7.4 Unconditional positive regard

- involves expressing a genuine caring for the patient
- conveys unconditional caring; it is not contaminated by evaluation or judgement of the patient's thoughts or feelings
- the attitude towards the client is not, 'I will accept you when' but rather 'I will accept you as you are'
- is the recognition of a patient's right to have feelings, though not the approval of all behaviour.

As in the case of genuineness, the concept of unconditional positive regard is often misconstrued as meaning an overly tolerant permissiveness where no boundaries are set. This is not the case. Rather, it refers to the fact that the acceptance and positive feelings that the counsellor has for the patient are not conditional upon the patient's actions or behaviours. This concept is particularly important in cases of skin disease where patients may feel that the way people feel about and act towards them is conditional upon how they look or how well they cope with their condition. Talking to a counsellor who is able to value the patient for who they are as a person as opposed to how they look or cope with their illness, may be sufficient to help empower them to see themselves differently and to make positive changes in their lives.

Patients often complain that health care professionals unaccustomed to seeing certain conditions appear shocked or uncomfortable when presented with someone with a disfiguring skin condition. It is important therefore that counsellors do not display shock or embarrassment when they first meet a patient who is obviously disfigured. Having to summon the courage to attend a counselling session is difficult enough for a patient, without feeling responsible for upsetting the counsellor. This may make it difficult for patients to disclose the extent of their despair, or feelings of feel shame or distress. If the counsellor can convey unconditional positive regard for the patients, they will be able to talk about their condition more openly, and not worry about whether or not their feelings are appropriate. The patient will be able to face and examine difficult feelings and issues while still feeling valued as a person, thus validating their experience and feelings.

Box 7.5 Empathic understanding

- implies that the counsellor will sense the client's feelings as if they were his/her own
- goes beyond the recognition of obvious feelings to the level of the less clearly expressed feelings of the patient
- can help patients discuss meanings and experiences about which they may be unaware

---

It is important to note that empathy is not sympathy, nor is it about acceptance, liking another person or agreeing with what they have said. Rather, it is the ability to understand what it is like to be where a person is, to understand what they are saying and to be able to reflect this. An accurate empathic response can help a person to understand and clarify what he or she is feeling and thinking about. A mere reflection, or parroting what the patient has said, may do little to further the patient's experience and may come across as condescending or repetitive. Psychologists have devised various methods of assessing the level of empathy in therapeutic reflections. Five levels of empathy described below illustrate how to reflect the patient's statements and feelings:

'Since the acne has gotten much worse, I've felt that nothing has gone right. People don't like me. I don't like my work. My relationship with my boyfriend has gone downhill. I don't like who I've become.'

A low-level of empathic response could be:

'It sounds like since your acne has gotten worse that things haven't been going well for you.'

This response is valid though it does not really attend to what the patient has said. It communicates less feeling than the patient has expressed. It has not helped the patient to gain insight into her experience of having acne.

A slightly more empathic response would be:

'So it seems that since it's got worse, the acne has made you feel quite negative about things.'

Although this statement conveys an awareness of the surface feelings of the patient, it dampens the meaning of what the patient has really said. The patient here is talking about the way her acne makes her feel and the counsellor responds with a statement about cognitive processing.

An empathic response that expresses what the patient has said may be as follows:

'It seems that what you're saying is that your acne has affected the way that you feel on several levels. It affects how you feel in your workplace, at home and even with your relationship with your boyfriend. It sounds like you feel that you don't even like who you are any more.'

This response captures what the patient has said. The response from the counsellor and the patient are almost interchangeable. The counsellor expresses the same feelings as the patient though they do not help the patient go deeper into her own experience.

An even more empathic response would be something like:

'I guess what you're saying is that when the acne gets worse it affects everything you do and everything you are. It's like there is no way to control it. It takes over, impacting how others see you and how you see yourself.'

This statement not only reflects what the patient has just said, but it also identifies feelings that the patient has not verbalized. This statement expresses meaning and emotion at a deeper level than the patient was able to express herself.

A 'level 5 response' is considered to be the most empathic response that a counsellor can make to a patient. In this case it might be along the lines of the following:

'It sounds like what you're saying is that when the acne flares up, that it's as if you have no control over parts of your life. It's as if when it gets worse

there is nothing you can do, it affects so many parts of your life at the same time that it just seems impossible to cope sometimes. It seems that what you're saying is when the acne gets worse, you don't only hate the way it looks, but that you don't like who you become.'

A response such as this adds to what the patient has said by expressing feelings that the patient was unable to express herself, and also by helping the patient to explore her experience at a deeper level.

Summarizing

Summarizing is a useful technique when counselling patients. It helps the counsellor to draw together what has been said and reflect to the patient 'the bigger picture' of what has happened during the session. It is important to note that, as is the case with empathic responses, the counsellor should be careful not to be too interpretive or to add too much new material to what is being said. Summarizing is about pulling together information to see how it fits, or does not fit, as the case may be (see Box 7.6).

Box 7.6 Summarizing

- drawing together feelings and observations made by the patient
- presenting the patient with a 'bigger picture' of what has been covered so far
- making salient any inconsistencies between feelings and observations that the patient has made and therefore allowing him/her to explore this
- helping the patient look at what has been covered in a more complete way and allowing him/her to make connections with regard to what has been said

---

Feeling that you are not doing enough

A common feeling amongst all counsellors, especially those who have only limited experience, is that they may not be doing enough to help the patient. They sometimes have the desire to ask a patient questions or provide them with useful tips on how to cope. However, the effect of the core skills described above on the patient and the counselling session should not be underestimated. Although other skills are important (and these are covered in the remaining chapters), they may not be well received by the patient if the core conditions are ignored.

Take for example the way that the empathic responses above were worded: *It seems like, I guess, You appear to be saying*. Each of these prefaces may appear to be merely reflecting what the patient has just said. But if delivered sensitively, these responses also convey respect to the patient. Although you may know more about counselling than the patients, they are the ones who know about their own experience! Empathy creates a climate in which the patient feels free to disagree with what the counsellor says and also empowers them to make changes in their lives which best suit their own circumstances.

Although the techniques described above are useful, it is appropriate that some patients and problems will require practical, concrete coping tools and interventions. A more directive approach to counselling can also be included where patients can be prompted to actively participate in behavioural and cognitive tasks that will help them to cope with particular situations. A detailed discussion of these techniques is outlined in the following chapters.

The use of counselling in dermatology

Before examining targeted and advanced psychotherapeutic interventions for people suffering from skin conditions, it is helpful to first consider the application of counselling to this population and the results of research associated with this.

Psychological treatment for people affected by a skin disease have ranged from psychoanalysis and the use of hypnosis (Gray and Lawlis, 1982) to cognitive and behavioural therapy (Wolpe, 1980). The literature contains some striking case examples of improvement of skin disease through the use of psychological interventions. One such example is that of a 16–year-old boy suffering from congenital ichthysioform erythrodermis or fish-skin disease (Barber, 1978). The condition had transformed the boy's skin into a thick black crust covered with small pimple-like elevations. The boy sought the help of a hypnotherapist who, through suggestion, was able almost entirely to eliminate the disease. Indeed, the results were sustained for years after treatment had ended. This is, of course, the description of a single case study and as there was no attempt to replicate it with other patients it is not possible to generalize the application of these findings to similar cases.

In their review of psychological therapies for the treatment of psoriasis, Winchell and Winchell and Watts (1988) describe a case in which two psychiatric patients with psoriasis, receiving the anti-depressant imipramine, were told that imipramine would have a beneficial effect on their skin condition. Following this suggestion, one of the patients experienced complete remission while the other improved considerably. These results were maintained in a four-month follow-up. In a similar case, a man with a 20–year history of psoriasis was treated by Frankel and Frankel and Misch (1973) using hypnosis and imagery. His condition improved significantly after several months of treatment and this was also maintained for several months. These studies describe specific cases in which no control groups existed and it is therefore important that the findings of this research are viewed in light of this.

Treatment methods have been reviewed for a number of skin diseases such as acne, puritus, psoriasis, eczema and virus-mediated diseases. The published literature suggests that psychological interventions have proven to be effective for each of these types of disorder (Brown and Fromm, 1987). However, there have been few systematically controlled investigations of their effectiveness and most of the data in this field comes from small-scale studies in which there is no control group. Stress-induced neuroendocrine changes have been found to adversely affect the immunity of patients suffering from skin cancer, and as a result may be implicated in high relapse rates. Psychological interventions, such as suggestion and hypnosis, have been shown to have the capacity to enhance immunity (Hall, 1982). Indeed such interventions have also been shown to improve immunologically mediated cutaneous conditions, such as chronic urticaria, dermatitis and viral warts (Barber, 1978; Rudzki et al., 1970; Surman et al., 1973). Behavioural and cognitive interventions have also been used in the treatment of dermatological conditions. Some researchers have helped patients with neurodermatitis to learn how to express anger and hostility in more functional ways (Schoenberg and Carr, 1963). Others maintain that successful treatment in these patients is directly linked to the patients' learning new coping methods which help them deal with their anger (Brown and Fromm, 1987). Psychotropic medication without psychotherapy has also been used in the management of skin conditions (Gupta and Vorhees, 1990; Gupta et al., 1987).

Although there is some evidence that psychological counselling can help patients cope with their condition, few investigations have been subjected to systematic investigation, and of those which have been published, a proportion have clear methodological shortcomings. These include a lack of appropriate control groups, small numbers of participants and a lack of counselling protocols which aid objective evaluations of outcomes (e.g. Brown and Bettley, 1971; Cole et al., 1988). There is a need for systematic evaluation to determine the efficacy of different approaches to counselling and the development of psychological treatments which focus on the unique issues faced by those suffering from cutaneous disease. Such investigations could take into account the personal, social and physical aspects of skin disease and seek to integrate these with factors such as cultural beliefs, the family system and the patient care system, so as to develop a holistic approach to counselling patients with cutaneous disease.

Conclusion

This chapter has provided an understanding of the central issues involved in counselling. Our definition of counselling was outlined and the potential benefits of counselling to dermatology patients were listed. An attempt was made to emphasize the importance of being aware of issues such as not belittling or minimizing the patient's experience. We then moved on to outline some core counselling skills that can be used with a dermatology population. The skills that were described highlighted the importance of the counselling relationship and how, through the application of empathy, genuineness and unconditional positive regard, patients can make positive progress in coming to terms with their problems. The idea that empathy is more than mere reflection was emphasized and examples of different levels and types of empathic responses were given. Finally the reader was provided with a brief overview of the literature regarding the use of counselling in dermatology.

8

Conceptual Ideas about Counselling People with Skin Disease

Introduction

In the previous chapter we considered the core skills of a counsellor and the application of these to dermatological problems. We now turn our attention to more advanced counselling skills and a deeper understanding of the relevant counselling and psychotherapeutic approaches in this and the remaining chapters. Some conceptual ideas about practising as a counsellor in a dermatology clinic or other settings in which patients are seen are described in this chapter. An ability to approach each new case and problem with a receptive openness and to recognize that each patient will require different therapeutic approaches and procedures is important. This attitude needs to be balanced with a level of competence in tried and tested counselling approaches and interventions.

An important distinction needs to be made between professional work with the patient (counselling) and work with other professionals caring for the patient (consultation and collaboration). Counselling in a health care setting should always involve both, even if it does not lead to face-to-face contact with the patient or family members. This is a basic tenet of a biopsychosocial systems perspective (Engel, 1977; McDaniel et al., 1992) which stresses the interaction and interrelatedness between disease, individual, family, health care providers and other biopsychosocial systems. The participation of a counsellor and the inclusion of the illness as a part of the interactional system results in a more comprehensive depiction of transaction and is illustrated in the Figure 8.1.

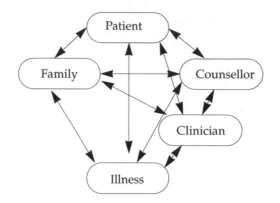

Figure 8.1: Pentagon depicting transactions which include a therapist in the system

Applying this framework helps to avoid the notion that a human problem is either a discrete physical or psychosocial problem. Instead, all problems are viewed as having biopsychosocial consequences. Psychosocial problems have physical components or features and physical problems have psychosocial ramifications. Inter-professional liaison is needed to ensure that problems (and solutions) are managed collaboratively. Providers of care, including counsellors, are viewed as part of, rather than apart from, the treatment system. This directly challenges the view that counsellors can remain neutral observers of their patients and detached from psychological processes. In these settings, counsellors may be confronted with complex interactions between different members of the system which develop into an intense emotional climate, especially in the face of pending loss or actual loss. This system can include a wide range of beliefs about illness and personal resilience which influence how people cope with other processes.

Considerations for counsellors working with dermatology patients

We have identified eight main considerations for the counsellor which reflect the unique and specific features of therapeutic work with patients suffering from skin disease. These are derived from different theories of counselling and psychotherapy (including psychodynamic, systemic, person-centered, cognitive-behavioural and personal construct, among others) and our own clinical experience. They are as follows:

1. Biopsychosocial approach

The application of a biopsychosocial approach (integrating biological, psychological and social features) to counselling has been extensively illustrated by McDaniel et al. (1992). There is a need for the counsellor to work collaboratively and without undue emphasis on either biological or psychological processes (to the detriment of the other). Social, medical and psychological events and processes are viewed as being interconnected and all require the ongoing attention of the counsellor. There is sometimes a tendency to over-emphasize psychological and social processes, whereas biomedical events may be equally relevant and themselves give rise to psychological problems. Put more simply, having a skin problem can cause distress and affect a person's self-esteem. Similarly, stress can cause skin problems. Different groups of professionals are sometimes taught to think about psychological problems in different and seemingly incompatible ways. Ailments of the mind and body are often conceptualized differently by counsellors, doctors and nurses. This has led to what has been termed the 'mind–body split'. The problem becomes more complex when treating patients whose symptoms appear to lie at the intersection of mind and body (somatoform disorders), such as those suffering from trichotillomania, parasitophobia and dermatitis artefacta (see Chapter 2).

2. Context

It is important to understand the context in which dermatological problems are identified or treated. The setting or context may be an in- or out-patient clinic, a GP surgery, a ward or private practice setting. Each will influence or constrain the amount of time available for the patient, the degree of privacy in counselling sessions and sometimes too the psychotherapeutic approach used. The context determines how problems are viewed, what can be done about them and who should be involved in treatment and care.

3. Beliefs about health and illness

Beliefs about health and illness are central to an understanding of how people are affected by their skin condition, how they may respond to their care and treatment, and how they are likely to cope. The cognitive behavioural approach emphasizes the relevance of cognitions and beliefs in the onset, maintenance and treatment of psychological problems. Wright et al. (1996) distinguish between constraining and facilitative beliefs in relation to health and illness. Constraining beliefs maintain problems and impede the search for new options or alternatives. Facilitative beliefs expand possibilities for solutions. Beliefs are directly linked to behaviour. If a patient does not believe that a particular prescribed medication is likely to clear up his acne, for example, it is less likely that he will comply with the treatment regime. The relevance of beliefs to counselling is discussed in more detail in the next chapter.

4. Attachment

The connection between attachment anxieties later in life and secure or insecure attachments to parents in infancy and childhood (Bowlby, 1975) helps us to understand how people relate to one another. The advent of illness can intensify, challenge or alter these patterns of attachment. A person suffering from a disfiguring skin condition may seek to maintain an emotional distance between himself and friends or potential suitors for fear of being rejected or feeling stigmatized. The affected individual may go to elaborate lengths to conceal the problem from others. High levels of anxiety may be associated with attempting to hide the skin condition. Not only does illness have the potential to threaten existing attachments (especially where there is the possibility of death), but illness can also give rise to new attachments, such as in the patient–health care provider relationship. John Byng-Hall (1995) has provided a solid foundation for understanding attachment in human relationships, especially in the context of changing family relationships.

5. Typology of illness

An understanding of the main characteristics of an illness is important in order to determine how a person may be affected (see Chapter 2). Rolland (1994) distinguished between four dimensions: onset, course, outcome and degree of incapacitation. It is not necessary to have an extensive understanding of a particular illness in order to offer counselling to an affected person, but it is important to appreciate the time phase (especially if it is a chronic illness) and practical consequences of the condition. This also helps to determine the possible ramifications for the patient's relationships. The location, size, contour and appearance of the skin condition may affect how the person copes with it. Similarly, a person's coping strategies will be influenced by temporal factors, such as whether it is a transient (relapsing) or permanent skin condition. Finally, treatment factors are also relevant (for example, whether the problem can be cured through treatment or medication).

6. Development and lifecycle

Developmental and lifecycle issues determine how an individual, couple or family are affected by skin problems. For an individual, this will depend on whether it is a newly born infant, child, adolescent, adult, and so on. Couples and families also progress through a series of developmental phases and each may imply or lead to changes in relationships between people. A newly wed couple, reconstituted family, or couple facing the 'empty nest' may each be affected differently in response to illness in the family. Carter and McGoldrick (1981) and Edwards and Davis (1998) have written extensively about the psychological impact of health problems at different stages of individual, couple and family development. A mother's attachment to her inconsolable infant son, for example, may be affected by his having eczema. She may blame herself for his condition and having to apply lotions to treat and soothe the patches may interfere with bonding. Similarly, an adolescent troubled by facial acne may lose confidence at a time when his peers are beginning to explore romantic relationships. While the symptoms may last no more than several months, it may do psychological damage to his self-esteem and confidence in making relationships.

7. *Cognition and behaviour*

The direct (and circular) relationship between cognition (thought) and behaviour (action) is central to an understanding of how problems are maintained and can be resolved. Many psychological problems or symptoms associated with health-related problems can be effectively treated with cognitive-behavioural therapy (Beck, 1976). Cognitive-behavioural therapy is especially useful when treating patients suffering from anxiety, depression, insomnia and other problems typically seen in mental health care settings, as well as for pain management, coping with itchiness and poor self-esteem arising from a skin problem. Identifying early experiences, dysfunctional assumptions, critical incidents, negative automatic thoughts and other factors which may maintain the problem are first steps towards its resolution. Thinking errors or **cognitive distortions** are often implicated in mood-related problems stemming from skin problems, hospitalization or a fear of undergoing medical procedures. For patients referred for counselling because of a fear of physical pain or separation from the family, behavioural methods (such as desensitization) can be used to ameliorate some symptoms.

8. *Time and timing*

Illness brings into sharp focus issues about time and longevity. The prospect of a reduced quality of life, or even a shortened life span if the condition is more serious, is often a source of psychological distress. Long-term counselling approaches may be neither desirable nor feasible in a context in which there is high demand for psychological care or where patients cannot regularly attend counselling sessions over a prolonged period because of their illness. Counsellors who work with these patients may be required to be flexible and to improvise, thereby remaining responsive to the patient's needs. Counselling sessions may need to be scheduled for when the patient attends for medical appointments. Furthermore, the pace of counselling must be adjusted to fit with the needs and coping abilities of the patient. Insensitivity on the part of a well-meaning counsellor may further distress the patient who in turn may lose confidence in the counsellor. One consequence may be the need to focus more on issues of timing in counselling. Some patients may not require a lengthy lead-in to counselling and may be willing and able to work at a deep level from the outset. Others, by virtue of their views about counselling, their problem, how they view themselves as coping and the natural employment of defences, may never benefit from the range of psychotherapeutic interventions that could otherwise have been employed. The challenge in these settings is for the counsellor to either work more quickly and intensively, or more slowly and cautiously. Some constraints may also relate to the physical setting, such as a lack of privacy or nowhere to sit comfortably when the patient is receiving treatment (such as under-going laser treatment), which may affect when sessions can be arranged and for how long they last.

Levels of counselling

It is useful to distinguish between different levels of counselling in order to illustrate the range of activities carried out by counsellors and also to help identify what 'mode' the counsellor may be engaged in at any time. Each one suggests a different relationship with the patient. For example, contrary to both some lay and informed beliefs about counselling, it is sometimes necessary for the counsellor to give information about treatment and care. This is usually in highly specialized settings or clinics where dedicated counsellors are part of a multidisciplinary dermatology team. The different levels of counselling should be viewed on a continuum rather than as discrete and unrelated activities:

1. *Information-giving*: the provision of factual information and advice about medical conditions, laboratory tests, treatments, drug trials, disease prevention, and health promotion among others.
2. *Implications counselling*: a discussion with the patient and/or others which addresses the implications of the information for the individual or family, and his or her personal circumstances.
3. *Supportive counselling*: in which the emotional consequences of the information and its implications can be identified and addressed in a supportive and caring environment.

4. Psychotherapeutic counselling: focuses on healing, psychological adjustment, coping and problem resolution.

Stages of counselling

There is wide variation in how counselling sessions are conducted and managed. They are usually in response to the needs and concerns of the patient, where the patient is seen, the context in which the counsellor works, and the counsellor's professional training. In health care settings where patients are physically ill, counsellors must be able to respond to and cope with a high level of unpredictability and emotional intensity. Ideally, a range of issues needs to be covered with patients in a first session, in a reasonably logical manner, progressing from one issue to the next.

Having a check-list in a first counselling session can help keep a focus by having a limited agenda. This is especially helpful where patients (a) are likely to be distressed, (b) are unfamiliar with counselling and therapeutic processes, (c) are likely to have multiple or complex issues that may need to be discussed and (d) may have only a single, one-off session or may be unable or unwilling to be followed-up.

The special circumstances and features of counselling in health care settings may mean that an initial consultation is possibly the only direct patient contact in some cases. Consequently, the counsellor needs to be adept in making an assessment and intervening all in the same session. Unlike in some other settings, patients may not benefit from follow-up because they may not want or need further sessions, or they may opt to be treated elsewhere and receive psychological support in another setting.

Conclusion

Different theoretical approaches contribute complementary ideas to the practice of counselling patients suffering from skin problems. The emphasis in counselling should be on developing an integrative approach, which brings together in a unifying conceptual framework different ideas and skills, rather than eclecticism which may seem confusing or muddled in practice. Experience teaches most practitioners to remain receptive to ideas developed outside their main theoretical framework and to integrate these into their practice.

9
Advanced Counselling Skills for Dermatology

Introduction

The importance of the counselling relationship has been explored and key issues in counselling have been outlined (such as attachment and patient beliefs) which underpin the dynamics of sessions. We have also listed different 'levels' of counselling as well as the various stages of the counselling process. However, the reader may feel that although the skills described up to this point are applicable to their work, there may be times where a more practical and intensive counselling approach is needed to help the patient. In this chapter, we build on the work described earlier and emphasize the usefulness of practical cognitive and behavioural techniques with dermatology patients.

Much of the work described in this chapter is based on a therapeutic approach known as Cognitive Behavioural Therapy (Beck, 1976). There are 3 basic beliefs which underpin this approach to counselling:

1. A person's emotions are determined by their thoughts or beliefs.
2. Emotional problems are a product of unrealistic, negative thoughts.
3. If negative and unrealistic thoughts can be changed, then emotional problems can be alleviated.

The focus in this approach is on examining and challenging negative thoughts which may stem from or lead to low mood or avoidance of certain situations or behaviours. Negative thoughts or cognitive errors include such things as disqualifying the positive aspects of an experience, jumping to conclusions and catastrophizing (these are discussed in detail later in the chapter). Negative thoughts or beliefs can be modified using a variety of techniques, for example, the counsellor might help the patient dispute the logic of some erroneous thoughts: 'How does it follow that your skin condition reflects something about you as a person?', or help patients to challenge the evidence of their beliefs: 'What is the evidence that everyone avoids you at parties because of your skin problem?' The counsellor might also ask the patient to carry out tasks that test out their beliefs. For example, a man who expresses apprehension about exposing his arms by wearing a T-shirt because he believes that strangers will be repulsed by his psoriatic lesions, might be encouraged to test out this fear through a small 'experiment' and report on what happens. If people do not stare at him, then this will have challenged his fear. If indeed they do stare, he could test the prediction that this would be 'a disaster' by examining what effect this had on him. It could also lead to a discussion about coping strategies such as thought blocking or distraction as well as coping skills. This could also include relaxation training and desensitization skills for coping with social anxiety (this is also discussed in detail later in the chapter).

Such an approach involves asking patients to monitor their thoughts both within and between sessions, so as to help them to learn to identify and challenge automatic negative cognitions. It can also involve the teaching of practical skills used to help counter negative social attention such as staring, being asked questions about one's condition and coping with comments from strangers and children.

The strategies discussed in this chapter can provide patients with a 'tool box' of practical coping strategies that they can use between counselling sessions and following the termination of the course of counselling. If these tools are used often enough and with success, then they are likely to become second nature to the patient and become integrated into their usual repertoire of behaviours.

Assessment

Patients find themselves in counselling through various routes. Some are referred by their GPs or dermatologists, others are encouraged or coaxed into it by family members while some self-refer. Depending on how they have reached the decision to attend for counselling, a patient's motivation to engage in the counselling process may vary and their expectations of the outcome may be over- or under-exaggerated. For example, patients who have decided to attend for counselling of their own volition, may have a different level of motivation from those who have been given an ultimatum by their partners to 'go and sort themselves out or else!' Patients who attend for counselling for the first time may be uncertain about what to expect and may feel anxious about what is expected of them during the counselling process. They may feel worried about the stigmatizing effects of being 'in therapy' or may feel guilty about having to seek help for something that is not life threatening and seemingly insignificant in the eyes of those around them.

The assessment session is a very important part of the counselling process. It enables the counsellor to establish a relationship with the patient, clarify any misconceptions that the patient might have about counselling and address any anxieties that the patient may have. It also provides a forum where the counsellor can explain what is involved in counselling and procedures such as completing questionnaires, self-reports and homework tasks. Most importantly, it is a context where the issues that the patient brings to counselling can be discussed and clarified. Their skin problem might be one of several issues that the person wants to work on, and the counsellor needs to be receptive to this. It is important that the counsellor also helps the patient to set realistic goals. Some patients may have excessively high expectations of what they can achieve and how quickly they can achieve it. For example, a patient who comes to counselling hoping that within a few weeks he or she will never again be troubled by others' reactions to their port-wine stain may be setting unrealistic goals for counselling. The counsellor might help that patient to tailor his or her goals to more realistic outcomes. Indeed, this might be considered the first major therapeutic intervention. Finally, the initial session is one where the patient should be made to feel safe, the issues of confidentiality discussed and any uncertainties or questions that he/she has about the counselling process addressed.

Helping patients to define their problem

A common problem that arises when working with patients with medical conditions is that counsellors make assumptions about the nature of the patient's problem and the way that it affects them. There is a danger of over-emphasizing certain issues while ignoring others that may be more pertinent to the patient. In order to avoid making assumptions, the counsellor should consider the following points:

- Allow the patient to explain what the issues are that have brought him/her to counselling. Try not to pre-empt the discussion by imposing your views about what their possible problems may be.
- Do not assume that the severity of the patient's condition will necessarily be related to the emotional problems that the patient is experiencing. Remember that many other factors, including social support and self-esteem, also affect how people adapt to their skin problem.
- The patient may not have previously had the opportunity to discuss their concerns with anyone so may not be sure about how to verbalize them. Do not assume that they will be able to 'open up' and discuss their feelings immediately; be patient and let them 'set the pace'.

In order to understand the definition of the patient's problem, the counsellor needs to acquire information about certain key areas regarding the patient's illness experience, namely:

- What the skin condition is, its course, duration and possible treatments that might be associated with it.
- How the condition affects them psychologically, are they coping with their condition, how has it affected their daily activities and their perception of themselves?
- Where counselling and treatment are offered, has the patient already discussed the psychological implications of their condition with other professionals? Has their perception of their problem been influenced by these discussions? Will the counsellor need to liaise with doctors or nurses regarding the patient's care?

It is important to address these issues. Lack of understanding about the patient's concerns by the counsellor can lead to problems such as the patient not keeping appointments, resisting counselling and problems between the counsellor and referrer. The counsellor should approach the patient and the problem in such a way that takes into account the complete picture of the patient's 'illness experience'.

Establishing what coping strategies the patient is using

Many patients who attend for counselling may have already attempted to solve certain problems. Their solutions may or may not have been successful. Indeed, in some situations it is the patient's attempted solution to the problem which becomes the main problem (Bor et al., 1998). For example, in the case below, the patient avoided sexual contact with others out of fear that they could discover that he had 'spots' on his penis. Avoidance can lead to social isolation and feelings of loneliness and the latter were the result of his attempted – though failed – solution and became the focus of counselling sessions.

Box 9.1 When the solution becomes the problem

'I recently developed these strange red spots on my penis and I hate them. The doctor said that they are nothing to worry about, but I have become so anxious about them that I have even tried scraping them off! I feel that they stop me from meeting people. I avoid having sex and I'm starting to feel really uncomfortable in any type of social situation. I try to deal with this by not going out that much and keeping to myself, but this is making me feel even more depressed and anxious.'

This patient's 'solution' to his problem (i.e. not going out) is actually compounding it. His anxiety about the spots on his penis is to a great extent anticipatory, that is, it is his anticipation of what might happen should someone see his penis that causes him to feel anxious and depressed. Counselling might help him to challenge the anticipatory anxiety and develop strategies to cope with them should they occur thereby 'inoculating' him against the symptoms of distress.

There are three main ways in which one can cope with a stressful situation:

- changing the situation out of which the stressful experience arises
- wearing clothes or make-up that hide the skin problem so as not to risk exposure and possible stigma
- challenging and altering the meaning of the stressful experience when it occurs; if people stare, one may acknowledge the fact that they might be staring for more reasons than their interest in the skin problem or that they are merely curious rather than repulsed
- controlling the effects of the stressful situation after it has occurred
- using coping skills for feelings of embarrassment or social phobia.

'Coping' is a dynamic process which relies on a range of strategies used at different times. These range from confronting risk and seeking social support to venting emotions and taking comfort in religious beliefs (Lazarus, 1993). In a review of coping strategies employed by people with some form of disfigurement the concept of coping was divided into the broad categories of: emotion-focused coping and problem-focused coping (Moss, 1997). The former deals with the way people attend to threat: That is, trying to change the way they think about a threat and their perception of it, so as to neutralize it or make it less threatening. An example of this is where patients challenge their perceptions of social situations when they feel that their physical appearance is being scrutinized. The latter involves doing something about it, such as employing practical tools for how to deal with staring, rude comments and how to confront other difficult social situations. These may include making eye contact with the other person, having a quick rehearsed response to rude comments, or changing the subject and diverting the other person's attention. In cases where a person can exert control over the threat, then problem-focused coping is effective, whereas in cases where the threat is not directly controllable, then emotion-focused coping is more useful. In most cases, both strategies are used both during and after a stressful event and the extent to which they prove to be useful will depend on the context in which they are used.

Strategies for facilitating change

Identifying negative thoughts or cognitive distortions

The beliefs that patients hold about their condition often influence how they cope with and adapt to it. Beliefs may be: 'I have done something bad to deserve this,' or 'My life is now ruined,' or 'Medical treatment will cure it,' among many others. A common feature amongst people who feel depressed or anxious is that they have negative, and at times seemingly irrational, thoughts about their life as a result of having their condition. These perceptions are often the result of 'errors in processing' whereby experiences and interpretations are distorted (Beck, 1976). Such 'cognitive errors' include:

- *elective abstraction*: attending only to negative aspects of appearance, so that the skin problem becomes the defining feature of the person's appearance: 'It doesn't matter that people say that I have a nice body or pretty eyes, the only thing that I notice about myself is the eczema.'
- *Personalization*: feeling responsible or upset about things that have nothing to do with oneself: 'The reason that she didn't sit next to me on the bus was because of my acne.'
- *Arbitrary inference*: reaching conclusions based on insufficient or inadequate evidence: 'The reason that he asked me to his party is because he feels sorry for me; there is no way someone would want to be nice to me when they can see how bad my psoriasis is.'
- *All-or-nothing thinking*: thinking in extremes: 'If I can't get to the point where I will never think about my port-wine stain again, then I'll never be happy.'
- *Generalization*: exaggerating the effect of an unpleasant experience so that it affects every aspect of one's life no matter how unrelated: 'My friend's 3–year-old daughter didn't want to touch my arm because of my psoriasis, therefore everybody must be disgusted by it.'
- *Catastrophizing*: thinking of only the worst case scenario and hugely exaggerating the effects of what might happen: 'If I go out without any make-up to cover up my port-wine stain, then everybody in the street will laugh and sneer at me and I won't be able to do the shopping that I have to do.'

It might be useful to first identify and then discuss these cognitive errors with patients and examine whether some of the conclusions that they have reached about their condition may be the result of these.

Use of questions in challenging thinking errors

One of the most useful ways to challenge negative or irrational thoughts is through questioning. Indeed it is more effective to elicit rational thoughts through the use of questioning than to encourage patients to think of 'rational' alternatives. By so doing, patients are encouraged to think through alternatives to their beliefs or responses rather than being told what to think. Questions facilitate the process between the patient and counsellor and help to achieve a structure to the session and:

• help to keep a focus on the problem and issue at hand
• explore/challenge ideas and hypotheses
• avoid making assumptions
• identify knowledge, concerns and wishes
• rank concerns and wishes
• help people to be specific by clarifying the meaning of what is said.

The way that the question is asked is also important. 'Why' questions are usually hard to answer (e.g. 'Why do you feel upset about having acne?') and may lead to vague and usually short responses, such as: 'I'm not sure,' or 'I don't know.' 'What' and 'how' questions are more useful, for example asking a patient: 'Why do you think that you feel anxious about people seeing the patches of eczema lesions on your legs?' may not be as useful as asking: 'What exactly do you think it is about others seeing your eczema patches that makes you anxious?'

Another useful questioning technique that helps to challenge negative thoughts are questions that try to get at the 'worst case scenario' that the patient anticipates. For example, a counsellor might ask a patient who is worried about other people noticing her psoriasis: 'What is the worst thing that you could imagine if someone was to see the patches on your arms?'

Patient: 'That they would stare at me and wonder what was wrong with my skin.'

Counsellor: 'Well let's assume that that's what would happen, why would that be such a terrible thing?'

Patient: 'I don't know, I guess I just hate the idea of people staring at me. It makes me feel uncomfortable, I never know what to do.'

Counsellor: 'Perhaps if we could work on some practical coping strategies together such as making eye contact with the person that is staring, or diverting your attention to something else, do you think that would be useful?'

Patient: 'Yes, that's my main problem you see, I never know what to do. If I had a way to deal with it then I wouldn't get so anxious when I thought about it.'

In some cases, patients are anxious about certain situations or events but do not understand why. By asking questions relating to 'worst case scenarios' the patient is challenged to examine their own thoughts and apprehensions and these can then be discussed during the session.

Thought monitoring

As mentioned earlier it is not situations in and of themselves that are stressful or depressing, but rather the perception that we have of them. If we learn first to identify negative or erroneous thoughts and then to challenge them, we can influence our interpretation of emotional reactions to various situations. Helping patients to become more aware of their thoughts can be achieved by asking them to record when they are feeling emotionally upset and the problem situations in which they find themselves. The counsellor first discusses with the patient the importance of attributions in how we feel and react in different situations. During the session, the counsellor might also discuss examples of negative or erroneous thinking that the patient has displayed during the session, and discuss with the patient alternative rationale responses to these thoughts.

For example:

Patient: I am really worried about going to my daughter's parent–teacher evening. I am convinced that the other parents and the staff at the school will notice these patches of dry skin on my face and avoid talking to me.

Counsellor: That sounds like quite an extreme reaction you are expecting. I wonder why you're expecting this to happen. Has this ever occurred before?

Patient: Well no, but I just feel that once they take a look at me, they won't like me because of the way I look.

Counsellor: I see. Is that the way that you usually decide if you like someone or not, or whether to talk to them?

Patient: Well no, of course not. But appearance is important.

Counsellor: Sure it's important, but so are a lot of other things including how friendly you are and how you relate to other people. Since you said that you don't make judgements about liking people based on the way that they look, is it likely that others do the same?

Patient: I guess so.

Counsellor: Also consider this, in all your past experience this extreme reaction you're expecting has never happened to you, right? Then how can you be certain that people will dislike you because of the appearance of your skin?

Patient: I see your point. Maybe I was exaggerating what I thought their response to me would be. No one has ever said, 'I hate you because of your skin' and I guess that most parents there will be anxious about meeting the teachers anyway and not too concerned about how everybody looks.

Once the patient is clear about the process, the counsellor can introduce the concept of monitoring thoughts for homework. The patient in this case was asked to complete a pre-printed thought monitoring sheet (see figure 9.1) and return with it to the next counselling session for discussion. It is important that clients fill in the sheet at the time that they are experiencing the emotional upset, or as close to it as possible so that they are more likely to accurately recall their negative thoughts.

actual or anticipated situation	negative automatic thoughts	emotion/ behaviour	alternative rational thoughts	emotion/ behaviour
Going to the gym, worried about having to wear T-shirt and shorts.	I am ugly and unattractive because of my skin and others will notice my eczema and think badly of me.	Anxiety, stress, sadness, despair.	Most people at the gym are conscious of their own bodies so they probably won't even notice me. Even if they do, it doesn't mean that they will think badly of me. Eczema is a skin condition and doesn't say anything about me as a person.	Relaxed, slightly low mood but not despair.

Figure 9.1: Thought monitoring

It should be noted that some conditions may be more stigmatizing in certain cultures than others, and therefore what may seem to be an irrational or negative belief from the patient's perspective may actually be valid within their specific context. It is important, therefore, that counsellors be aware of such cultural differences and take account of these in their discussions with patients. For example, in some parts of India, vitiligo is seen to be a sign of karmic punishment. Therefore a patient who conveys the belief that they are bad and people will not like them because they have vitiligo may be doing so because this idea has been reinforced by the sociocultural environment in which they live.

Thought blocking

Thought blocking is a technique commonly used with people suffering from obsessive disorders. It provides a means of dismissing intrusive thoughts and thus reducing their duration. In the case of skin disease, recurring thoughts regarding one's appearance are common. Even though these are not likely to be classified as obsessive, patients nevertheless often find themselves becoming overly anxious regarding how others react to the way that they look and may engage in checking behaviours to see whether the size, number or shape of their lesions has changed. In order to help patients cope with these recurring thoughts and reduce the frequency of checking behaviours, a technique known as thought blocking may be used.

The patient is initially asked to describe the different recurring thoughts that they have and when and where these tend to take place. The counsellor then explains to the patient that they will describe one of these situations and that as soon as he or she begins having the recurring thought to put a hand up. As soon as the patient has raised the hand, the counsellor shouts 'Stop'! The patient is then asked what happened to the thought, which should have disappeared. This is then repeated with different thoughts that the patient has identified until he/she feels ready to try 'stopping' the thoughts on their own. When in public it will be of course be difficult for patients to shout 'Stop!' out loud, so as an alternative they may opt to wear a rubber band around their wrist and to snap it sharply when they begin to feel the recurring thought coming on. Thought stopping should be practised as homework, and any difficulties identified and reported back to the counsellor (Hawton et al., 1994).

Distraction

Another means of controlling anxiety due to negative thoughts is through the use of distraction. This technique is often used when patients find themselves becoming anxious or distressed in a particular situation. If, for example, they begin to feel anxious while on a bus because they are worried that others can see their acne scars, then they may use distraction as a means to help them divert their attention from the anxiety-provoking thoughts or stimulus. There are several ways that this can be done. First, the patient may be asked to focus their attention on a neutral event or object. They may be asked to count how many people on the bus are wearing blue sweaters or how many cars overtook them in the last five minutes. Second, mental exercises may be used, such as reciting the alphabet backwards or counting to one thousand in multiples of 13. Finally, another useful technique involves asking patients to recall in detail a pleasant memory or fantasy that they may have. This may be a recent holiday or dreaming of what they would do if they won the lottery. Through the use of distraction, the patient is then able control their anxiety and this in turn prevents a vicious cycle from building up whereby negative thoughts make the patient anxious and this anxiety further exacerbates negative thoughts.

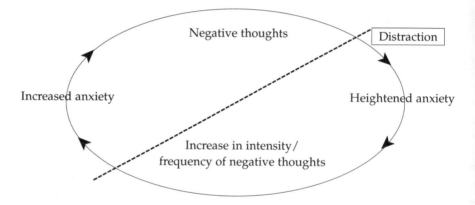

Figure 9.2: Vicious cycle set up by negative thoughts and how distraction can help break the cycle

Relaxation

Relaxation is a useful way to help patients prepare for anxiety provoking situations or to cope with stressful social predicaments. Relaxation can be used on its own as a means to reduce anxiety and tension, or can be paired up with imagery to help patients prepare for potentially difficult or stressful situations. There are various different techniques that can be used; the method we describe below is based on Ost's applied relaxation training (Ost, 1987). The series of relaxation steps is as follows:

1. The initial stage of this training involves teaching patients to distinguish between tension and relaxation that they feel in their bodies. Through this, they learn to become aware of when they are feeling

tense. The patient is asked to sit in a comfortable chair while the counsellor models how muscles can be tensed and relaxed by clenching and relaxing jaws, tensing and releasing fists etc.
2. The patient is asked to close their eyes and the counsellor begins to take the patient through the various muscle groups, beginning from the face and moving down to the shoulders, neck, arms, torso and legs.
3. The patient is asked to maintain the tension for approximately five seconds and then relax the same muscle group for approximately ten seconds. This is done for each muscle group.
4. After finishing all the muscle groups the patient is asked to rate how relaxed he or she feels from a scale from one to a hundred.
5. The counsellor checks whether or not the patient has had any problems with a particular muscle group and if so he or she is helped to work through this.
6. Patients are asked to practise progressive relaxation daily and keep a record of the time taken to relax and the extent of relaxation achieved on a scale of one to a hundred.

As a patient becomes more accustomed to using progressive relaxation, the time taken to relax can be reduced by omitting the tension exercises.

Using imagery to cope with anxiety-provoking situations

The concept of employing imagery to help people cope with anxiety relating to the skin condition is based on the principal that if you can prepare for a situation which you predict will be stressful or anxiety-provoking, you should be able to cope better with it. In the case of people with skin disease, this can be useful when helping them prepare for either an event or activity that they are anxious about. A useful technique is to help the patient visualize the feared situation while in a relaxed state. If the patient can feel relaxed while imagining the feared stimulus, then it is more likely that they will be relaxed when the actual situation occurs. Below are some important steps in helping patients prepare for anxiety-provoking situations:

- Establish with the patient what exactly the feared stimulus is and what about it makes them feel anxious. For example, they might say that they are worried about being seen in a swimming costume for the first time because of psoriasis, but may be more anxious about friends seeing them than strangers or vice versa. By establishing the exact nature of your patient's anxiety, you will be able to tailor the visualization exercise to address this.
- Help your patient to relax by asking them to sit comfortably, and to become aware of any tension they are feeling in their muscles (see section above on relaxation). Speak slowly and clearly and make

sure there are no interruptions while this is happening.

- While the patient is in the relaxed state, ask him or her to imagine the feared scenario, giving as much detail as possible regarding the location and what is happening. For example, ask them to describe where they will be swimming, who will be there, what their swimming costume is like etc. Throughout your description, check how anxious or nervous they feel, reassuring them that they are safe and reminding them to breath steadily and relax.
- Help the patient to visualize how he/she might react to the feared stimulus/situation and give realistic suggestions as to what might happen. For example your patient might be especially worried about children pointing at them. Give suggestions about possible responses that they can make to the children, and suggest likely outcomes to these responses. Keep monitoring the patient's state of relaxation and breathing.
- Finally, end the visualization by asking the patient how they feel and check with them what the visualization exercise felt like and whether they thought it was useful. They may also be given an 'intrusive thought' to repeat to themselves outside of the session to maintain the effects. This could be in the form of a mantra such as: it may feel a bit anxiety-provoking and this may be uncomfortable but anxiety of this kind is not dangerous.

Once the patient feels that he/she is comfortable with the visualization exercise, you can begin discussing the possibility of trying out an exercise between sessions. A woman who starts off visualizing what it would feel like to wear a sleeveless dress that reveals her depigmented skin might eventually be able to do so more comfortably because she has anticipated what her emotional and cognitive reactions to this might be, has coping strategies she can use and has prepared for these.

Remembering positive aspects about appearance

Another technique that can be useful is asking patients to think of, and list, positive aspects of their appearance. So much emphasis may have been placed on their skin condition that it becomes all that patients see when they look in the mirror. They may ignore the fact that prior to the onset of the condition they liked certain aspects of their appearance. They may focus instead only on the skin disease and minimize the importance of other bodily features or indeed the importance of their body as something more than just an aesthetic object. If this is the case, patients can be asked to 'look past the skin disease' and identify what parts of their appearance that they are happy with. Doing this can help them to be reminded that they are more than their skin problem and that their appearance may be attractive in other ways.

Graded exposure

The fear and apprehension that a person feels about themselves and others may dominate all aspects of their lives. In the same way that a person with a phobia about snakes may avoid anything associated with the feared stimulus (e.g. zoos, television nature programmes, photographs that feature snakes). The same may apply to patients with skin disease. For example, they may cover up their skin with make-up or clothes that conceal the condition, avoid conversations about appearance or avoid activities where there is a possibility of others noticing their condition. One way to help patients cope is by helping them to challenge their beliefs about the feared situation through graded exposure. This involves first establishing with the patient what the feared stimulus is and then constructing a hierarchy of situations that the patient avoids. Only those situations that the patient wishes to make goals are entered on the list. The procedure generally involves the following:

- establishing with the patient what the feared stimulus is: e.g. being seen in public without camouflage make-up to hide vitiligo lesions
- constructing a hierarchy with the client of less feared situations that could lead up to this, such as
  - not wearing make-up when at home alone
  - not wearing make-up in front of partner
  - not wearing make-up when friends come to visit
  - going out to get the morning paper without make-up
  - going out for a drive with no make-up on
  - going to a public place/event without make-up
- asking the patient to rate the degree of difficulty that she would experience undertaking each of the items on the list from 0–100, where 0 indicates 'no difficulty' and 100 indicates 'the most difficult':

	(1–100)
- degree of difficulty	
- not wearing make-up when at home alone	30
- not wearing make-up in front of partner	50
- not wearing make-up when friends come to visit	90
- going out to get the morning paper without make-up	70
- going out for a drive with no make-up on	80
- going to a public place/event without make-up	100

- Once the patient has rated the various activities or situations in order of difficulty, the activities or situations are then put into ascending order of least difficult to most difficult and the patient is then asked to undertake the least difficult activity on the list.
- Once the patient has mastered coping with the least anxiety-provoking situation, and can do so comfortably, he or she is then asked

to move up the list, doing the same with each situation until reaching the most difficult task at the top of the list. By doing this, the patient is able to challenge negative or irrational thoughts, disproving those beliefs that led to the avoidance of the different situations. relaxation training can be added to the exercise to help the patient address each task and do so feeling more emotionally settled and comfortable.

Homework

Homework tasks can prove a useful tool in counselling. They should be devised to enable patients to practise and master counselling interventions (e.g. countering negative thoughts, relaxation). They may be asked to keep a diary of their thoughts regarding their condition, or to practise relaxation techniques, and report back on their progress in subsequent sessions. It is important that the homework task is discussed and agreed upon by both patient and counsellor. This way, the task is more likely to be relevant to the patient's problems and therefore the patient is more likely to be motivated to carry it out.

Once the homework task has been decided upon, the counsellor needs to clarify what should be done, where and how many times. It is also important that the counsellor ensures that the patient understands the reason behind doing the homework. Finally, the counsellor assesses the patient's commitment to carrying out the homework. The counsellor might ask, for example, whether or not the patient can foresee any difficulties in carrying out the task. These might be either practical, such as, 'I would like to try going out with a short-sleeved shirt, but its been raining and cold so I can't' or reflect resistance, 'I just can't see myself going out without completely covering up my legs.' If problems are identified the counsellor can address them with the patient or focus on them more in the counselling sessions before assigning them as homework tasks.

Putting these techniques into practice

Many counsellors working in health care and dermatology settings are required to offer a focused and time-limited course of counselling. Figure 9.3 illustrates how the ideas described thus far can be adapted for use in eight 50–minute sessions. This protocol has been successfully used with dermatology patients (Papadopoulos et al., 1998).

Table 9.1: Protocol for time-limited counselling

Assessment session
- demographic data and family history gathered from the subject
- subject questioned on their beliefs regarding the onset, course and meaning of the condition
- subject asked what issues they feel will need to be addressed during counselling
- subject asked what expectations they have from counselling
- importance of following homework assignments and giving feedback to therapist explained
- issues of confidentiality discussed
- an explanation of CBT given

Session 2
- issues regarding the onset of the condition discussed/patient's beliefs regarding the illness examined
- patient's experiences following the onset of the illness discussed, patient asked to identify any experiences that they found particularly stressful and why
- patient asked what the worst thing about having skin disease is, both in a real and in an imagined case scenario, possible ways to face such scenarios examined
- relaxation techniques which patient can use when faced with stress or anxiety about the condition discussed
- for homework subject asked to keep a daily record of when the skin condition has stopped them from doing something they wanted to do and to record their thoughts about this

---

Session 3
- discuss previous week's homework
- discuss what coping mechanisms the patient has found useful when having to deal with condition
- discuss camouflage make-up and when this is used, see if patient feels comfortable being seen without make-up and why
- construct with patient a hierarchy of body parts (moderately satisfied to least satisfied), use anxiety reduction techniques thinking about each part of the body specifically and then the overall body
- do relaxation and imagery of feared situation
- for homework ask patient to continue with daily diary of thoughts related to skin condition, and to identify a recent occasion where they felt that the condition was stopping them from participating in a activity

Session 4
- discuss previous week's homework
- ask patient to look at depigmented part of their body and speak automatic thoughts that come to mind – help patient identify alternative thoughts, ask patient to reinforce him/herself for identifying these thoughts
- ask patients to discuss any incidents in which they felt they were being stared at or talked about, ask patients to think of alternative reasons why they may have been stared at, discuss practical ways of coping with staring
- explore if anything positive had come out of the illness
- for homework ask patient to report experiences in which they felt that their condition was being spoken about or was stopping them from doing things,ask them to think of alternative reasons for what happened in the same way as was discussed in the session

Session 5
- discuss previous week's homework
- ask patient to describe two situations which they generally avoid when upset about their appearance
- ask subject to predict what might happen when faced with these situations
- ask patient to write down rational beliefs to negative predictions
- go through relaxation with patient and use imagery regarding the removal of camouflage make-up
- for homework ask patient to take off camouflage makeup/or clothing used to hide lesions and look in the mirror for 1–2 minutes, ask patient to record feelings following this activity, ask patient to practise relaxation techniques discussed during session

Session 6
- discuss previous week's homework
- introduce subject to the concept of engaging in behaviours that give a sense of mastery or pleasure to help them view their body for its capabilities and not only for its relevance as an aesthetic object
- ask patient what their thoughts are about this
- for homework ask subject to rate the frequency of involvement in physical activities and rate these activities in terms of mastery and pleasure
- for homework ask patient to enter one of these situations while thinking of rational beliefs and rehearsing positive thoughts
- remind patient of ending in two weeks and discuss any stresses that they may have

Session 7
- discuss previous week's homework
- discuss degree of handicap: social/occupational/leisure they feel associated with the condition
- discuss changes in lifestyle that have been made since the onset of illness
- ask patient to speak about themself and their lives without mentioning their condition
- address any stresses patient has in terms of ending treatment
- for homework ask patient to write out counter-arguments for beliefs regarding illness

---

Session 8
- review homework from previous session
- review basic components of programme and techniques for post-treatment maintenance gains
- review any improvement subject has made and discuss stress inoculation and relapse prevention procedures

---

Maintaining changes derived from counselling sessions

Towards the end of counselling, the patient might express concern about how he or she will cope having left the safety of the counselling environment and may feel uneasy about how well they will be able to put the benefits of counselling into practice and to maintain these. These concerns should not be dismissed. Endings in counselling have the potential to either reinforce change or undo the gains achieved. It is important to reassure the patient that it is 'normal' or 'expected' that there will be some level of relapse in some situations. This may be because their confidence slips or they become anxious that they do not have the safety of the counselling sessions in which to talk about their concerns. Predicting some relapse and providing some reassurance about this is an important and helpful therapeutic intervention in itself. Some additional strategies for helping patients end therapy are outlined below:

- prepare the patient for the end of therapy by a reminder in the last few sessions leading up to the end that the course of counselling will be drawing to a finish
- remind the patient of the gains made during the course of counselling. If they have kept a diary, look over it together comparing how they felt at the beginning of counselling and how they feel now
- discuss with the patient the importance of continuing to carry out

the challenges to negative thoughts, relaxation techniques or whatever else the patient found useful during counselling
- remind the patient that although you spent time together working
  on the problem, the majority of the time the patient worked at it
  alone and therefore the patient is the most important part of the
  counselling process.

Conclusion

Researchers have reported some measure of success with helping
people with disfigurements and skin disease cope with their problems
through counselling. Some have been in the form of structured groups
run for disfigured individuals, where social skills training was an inte-
gral part of the group process (Robinson et al., 1996). Others have
reported success with the use of cognitive-based therapies for people
with body image disturbance (Cash, 1990). Unfortunately, the importance of comprehensive and specialist psychological care in the treatment process is often overlooked by those who work in this field.
Although some health care settings offer patient-led self-help groups
or befriending schemes where new patients are given the chance to
meet old patients, rarely do they have the opportunity to engage in
counselling with trained professionals. This chapter has attempted to
describe how advanced counselling skills can be applied in working
with dermatology patients. Different therapeutic techniques, including thought monitoring, visualization and the use of questions were
discussed and suggestions were made for how these could be tailored
to a dermatology population. Significant improvements can be made
in how dermatology patients cope with and adapt to their illness
through psychological counselling using the skills described above.

10

Counselling Dermatology Patients Who Have Psychosomatic Problems

Introduction

Some patients are either not reassured by their GP or dermatologist that they do not have an identifiable medical problem, or they have a medical condition but have become somatically fixated. They are respectively referred to in the literature as the 'worried well' or somatizing patients. The problem directly affects the relationship between the doctor, patient and family. The impasse and consequent feelings of exasperation and hopelessness often result in negative views developing about these patients who are perceived as wilful, resistant to change, rigid in their thinking, and a drain on professional and personal resources. These patients may be diagnosed as having trichotillomania (pulling out their hair), parasitophobia (an erroneous belief that their skin is infested with a parasite), dermatitis artefacta and neurotic excoriations among others. Other patients who fall under this category are those whose skin condition is exacerbated by social conditions or emotional problems (for example some patients being treated for eczema) but who either reject this interpretation or who fail to act on the advice of their doctor or nurse.

We recognize the difficulties presented by these patients because they are especially challenging but also view them as an opportunity to work collaboratively with the patient, family and professional colleagues and to try innovative approaches to treating the problem. Counsellors can gain acceptance as a member of the health care team through successful treatment of these cases. Professional colleagues usually recognize that these patients are time-consuming and can leave doctors and nurses feeling exasperated.

Theoretical concepts

Abnormal illness behaviour (such as hypochondriasis) is regarded as a syndrome of mental illness in psychiatry. The diagnosis is made when there is a perceived discrepancy between the patient's reaction to a medical problem and the nature of the medical problem, if indeed there is one (Mayou, 1989). A prerequisite for making this diagnosis is that the patient has been thoroughly investigated by a doctor. Furthermore, laboratory tests and diagnostic procedures must have been accurately carried out so the patient's responses can be considered against objective criteria. Nevertheless, patients are prone to making subjective interpretations of their condition which may be at variance with the opinions of health care professionals who rely on the results of objective diagnostic procedures and laboratory tests. Where patients' conceptualizations of their skin condition, illness or symptoms differ from those of health care professionals, there is the potential for an impasse to occur in the relationship. This chapter describes how to identify and manage this impasse in counselling sessions.

These patients use somatic language to describe their difficulties, irrespective of whether or not these are physical or emotional problems (McDaniel et al., 1992). The cause and nature of rashes and skin problems may be construed differently by the patient and doctor. The attending doctor may attempt to reassure the patient or to offer a psychological explanation (for example, 'these patches on your skin are a sign of stress rather than cancer'). However, reassurance is usually rejected. The 'worried well' may fear that they have contracted a particular skin condition or they may complain that they already have signs and symptoms of disease, while there may be no medical evidence for this or the evidence suggests that the problem is primarily a psychological one. The range extends from those who misinterpret somatic signs and then worry about their health (for example, those who believe that their skin rash indicates that they have a more serious internal problem) to patients with somatic delusions that can even mimic 'real' symptoms, such as in the case of parasitophobia.

Most people will at some time have transient worries about their health and minor symptoms. However, a small group of patients become fixated by these symptoms and worry about them incessantly. These patients are most likely to be referred to counsellors after doctors have failed to reassure them, in spite of repeated and logical explanations. They may be labelled as 'hypochondriacal', 'compulsive', 'obsessive' or 'hysterical'. Such labels rarely help to break the cycle of help-seeking behaviour and are not reassuring to the patient. The patient's drive for help and the doctor's response to this can be depicted as follows (see Figure 10.1).

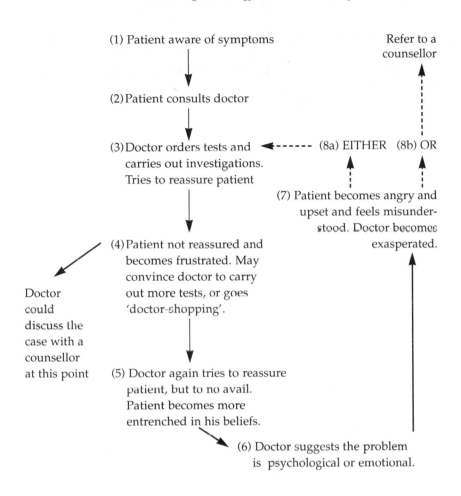

Figure 10.1: Cycle of doctor–patient interaction in 'worried well' case

The onset of the patient's worry may coincide with feelings of anxiety, depression or guilt. Counselling sessions frequently focus on uncovering possible 'causes' of the patient's disproportionate and unremitting worry, vigorously exploring the link between emotional problems and their somatic expression. The suggestion to the patient that somatic symptoms may be indicative of emotional problems is, however, often rebuffed. This is because somatic symptoms:

(a) are a more socially acceptable presentation of problems and carry less stigma than psychological problems
(b) are viewed by the patient as physical (and consequently, amenable to diagnosis and treatment)
(c) can lead to secondary gains for the patient in the form of attention from increasingly frustrated professional and non-professional caregivers.

Pointing out these processes to the patient rarely alleviates the symptoms. The patient will deny consciously misconstruing his symptoms, and this can lead to a more polarized relationship between the patient and the doctor or counsellor. There is sometimes an ebb and flow in the patient's experience of these problems and consequently the tenacity with which the conviction, or delusion, is held.

Events and psychological processes in the patient's life may be associated with a tendency to display psychosomatic manifestations of distress, including:

1. Those with relationship problems

A fear of illness can indicate difficulties about entering into, remaining in and ending relationships. The worry is a symptom which regulates the social and emotional distance in a relationship. For example, a lonely person may find some relief from solitude because caregivers take their skin complaint seriously. The somatic presentation of a psychological problem may be viewed as a less stigmatizing means of gaining access to treatment and through which there is less risk of rejection for the patient. Thus, an intractable worry about one's health may signal a call for professional help in a troubled relationship.

2. Individuals, couples and families going through life-cycle transitions

Points of transition in an individual's, couples', and family life cycles may exacerbate existing stress and relationship difficulties, which may be expressed as somatic problems such as eczema. Examples are parents of rebelling adolescents, couples facing the 'empty nest', individuals experiencing mid-life crises, people who have suffered recent bereavement and those who have recently divorced or separated.

3. Those with past medical or psychological problems, or who have some connection with health care

There may be an elevated risk for these patients because of their personal experience of health care. Those who have previously been treated for medical problems may be more likely to somatize than those who do not have a past medical history.

4. Misunderstandings of health education messages

A small 'worried well' group comprises those who may have misunderstood health education messages and believe themselves to be at risk or illness because of lifestyle, exposure to an infectious agent in foreign countries, or messages about self-diagnosis (such as melanomas resulting from too much exposure to the sun). Public health education through mass media campaigns (television, radio, newspapers) convey only limited information. Some may then need to have a personal interview with an informed counsellor or health professional for their specific questions and anxieties to be addressed.

Managing the 'worried well': the counsellor's dilemma

It is useful to have an overview of the management of these patients. The term 'worried well' is an inaccurate definition for patients who are self-referred or have not previously seen a doctor. No patient referred for counselling can be defined as well by a counsellor until he has been examined and investigated by a doctor. Only once physical illness has been excluded can the patient be viewed as 'worried' and 'well'. Any worry about a patient's health should be taken seriously and it is essential to defer to medical colleagues to first address the problem.

A problem arises where the patient is not reassured by the doctor. If the counsellor then colludes with the patient's definition of the problem, he may reinforce the patient's problem. If, on the other hand, the counsellor tries to reassure the patient, he will be doing precisely what the doctor has already tried, and failed, to achieve. Although reassurance may temporarily alleviate the patient's worries, it is unlikely to solve the underlying problem. A more effective approach is for the counsellor to simultaneously present both sides of the dilemma, and to do so tentatively. This means on the one hand accepting the patient's view of himself suffering from a physical illness, whilst at the same time cautiously introducing the possibility that these concerns about his health must be anxiety provoking and stressful for the patient. This opens up the possibility for further discussion with the patient about the impact of illness. Developing these ideas within the counselling relationship helps to broaden the patient's view of his so-called illness without incurring the patient's resistance to being labelled as having a purely psychological problem.

Care must be taken to avoid directly interpreting the patient's behaviour exclusively in psychological terms at an early stage in the counselling relationship. Interpretation of the problem sometimes has negative connotations and may lead the patient to feel rejected and misunderstood, resulting in more help-seeking behaviour and even ending the counselling relationship. Equally, there is a possibility that seeing the patient for counselling in a health care setting, over a prolonged period, could inadvertently reinforce the problem by exposing the patient to a medical context.

Guidelines for counselling the 'worried well'

The referral and first stages of counselling

The importance of the referral process is particularly relevant with somatizing patients. Most of these patients are unreceptive to a referral to a counsellor, which is entirely congruent with the nature of how they view their problem.

- They believe they have a physical rather than a psychological problem.
- The patient's anger, annoyance or dejection may be increased by the doctor's suggestion of a referral.
- The patient may feel abandoned and misunderstood, relegated to being emotionally disturbed, and annoyed at the suggestion that his symptoms are either exaggerated or feigned.
- The patient may strongly resist a referral by intensifying the pursuit for a medical diagnosis, becoming more demanding of the doctor or by seeking second and subsequent opinions from other specialists.
- They may even feign co-operation to project a receptive openness to any 'medical' investigations and to avoid being combative with the doctor, confirming suspicions of psychological difficulties (Turk and Salovey, 1995). Even if the patient is not outwardly defensive and 'resistant' to the referral and seems co-operative, the counsellor should assume that he or she may not be willing to begin to view his or her problem in psychological terms.

The first meeting with the patient is more likely to be successful if it includes the referring doctor, even if this is only for a part of the session (see Chapter 12 on models of collaboration). Discussion between the counsellor and doctor before the meeting can facilitate the referral. Seeing the patient in this first meeting in the doctor's consulting room prevents an abrupt shift in focus from the physical to the psychological. It conveys the counsellor's initial acceptance of the patient's medical definition of the problem. The presence of the doctor and counsellor can also help to demystify the counselling process for the patient by clarifying what might be achieved through counselling. This can be achieved by: the doctor introducing the counsellor as a part of the clinical team, reinforcing the mind–body link;

- emphasizing the counsellor's expertise in helping people to cope better with illness and medical procedures, including knowledge of specialist skills to help them with their self-esteem, disruption to their life, relationships, distressing emotions (such as anxiety and resentment) and changes in roles and lifestyle;
- reassuring the patient, at this stage, that medical concerns will con-

tinue to be dealt with by the doctor and that the counsellor and doctor will exchange information about the client's condition and progress.

All these details can enhance the chances of counselling having some positive effect on the patient's condition.

Counselling should start by getting the patient's view of his problem. Thereafter, acknowledging the devastating effects of the patient's symptoms or condition on his or her life can be a way of building rapport. This should include some discussion about the impact of the symptoms on the patient's relationships and career, and intrusion into leisure activities. The history of the onset, symptoms, significant events and medical investigations should also be addressed. It is important to gradually limit discussion of this from session to session, otherwise the counsellor may inadvertently reinforce the patient's somatic fixation.

The main emphasis in the initial stages of counselling is to acknowledge the patient's distress, to resist the temptation to reassure the patient and to avoid offering psychological interpretations. This is achieved by assuming a collaborative and non-oppositional stance and by using medical language and medically-styled interventions in counselling (McDaniel et al., 1992). These may include desensitization interventions, symptom diaries and attention to the patient's sleep, diet and exercise routines. The counsellor should ask affirming questions about how the patient has coped with these symptoms and other unwelcome experiences and events in his life. Where possible, routine problem-defining questions should be asked which help the counsellor to construct a wider map of the problem.

Some of the following questions can help the counsellor to explore these issues with the patient

- When did this problem start?
- What do you think has caused this problem?
- What do you think the symptoms are a sign of?
- What have you done to help alleviate the symptoms? With what effect?
- Who else knows about this problem? And what are their views about it?
- Have you had other medical problems in the past? How did these affect you?
- What was happening in other areas of your life (e.g. relationships, work) when your worries/symptoms started?
- How have these concerns affected you (emotionally)?
- How have other health care providers been of help to you with this problem? (Always frame the question positively even if you suspect that the patient will criticise them for not taking him seriously.)

- How do you see your ideas about your symptoms being similar to or different from your doctor's ideas about them?

At the end of the initial stage of counselling, the patient should have had an opportunity to talk about their view of the medical problem and the impact this has on them. Unlike in some other counselling situations, it may not be possible to discuss and agree on specific treatment goals. The reason for this is that the patient is likely to re-emphasize their somatic concerns, thereby diminishing the place of counselling in their treatment.

Main therapeutic interventions

Innovative therapeutic interventions are required to deal with an impasse that is likely to arise between the counsellor and patient in the course of counselling. It mirrors that which has arisen between the patient and the doctor. An impasse is marked by a 'more-of-the-same' situation (Watzlawick et al., 1974) in which any intervention by the counsellor results in 'no change' in the patient. In counselling a somatically fixated or 'worried well' patient, a symmetrical relationship between the counsellor and patient can develop, characterized by an increasingly authoritative stance by the counsellor trying to convince an equally rigid patient that he is not ill, but to no avail.

Patient:	⟶	Counsellor:
'These symptoms must indicate that I am ill.'	⟵	'The doctor says that all the tests are negative, so you must be well.'

This can become a 'game without end', with some variations, depicted in the above diagram. The interaction becomes repetitive and ineffective. Traditional theories about resistance in psychotherapy tend to blame the patient for the impasse. The counsellor may indicate what he perceives as the patient's resistance; or he may slightly vary his interactive behaviour, for example, by raising his voice or adopting a tone of greater authority. The view we take about resistance (be it to the doctor's opinion or to prescribed treatment) is derived from Kelly's (1969) work in psychotherapy. He suggests that the impasse between the counsellor and patient reflects the 'stuckness' of the counsellor rather than the obduracy of the patient. In other words, the counsellor has not found the right 'key to the door'. To resolve this, the counsellor needs to become creative (and less predictable) in his problem-solving, rather than blaming or labelling the patient.

Cognitive-behavioural methods of intervention aimed at changing the patient's beliefs and behaviour and developing coping stress skills can be used (Turk and Salovey, 1995). These interactions assume a fit between the patient's conceptualization of their problem and the rationale for the treatment being offered. As the patient is unlikely to accept that somatizing is a symptom of a psychological problem, he may resist cognitive-behavioural interventions until such time as his conceptualizations change. For this reason, they may be only partially successful with a limited number of these cases. None-the-less, cognitive and behavioural interventions can be used in the course of a wider treatment especially reinforcement (of more adaptive illness responses), exposure (to feared situations), extinction (of inappropriate illness behaviours), fostering self-control (over maladaptive thoughts, feelings and behaviours), as well as biofeedback, relaxation training and distraction skills training.

The overall aim is to shift the patient's cognitive and behavioural repertoire away from habitual and rigid automatic thoughts and responses. A key feature is that the patient's physical and psychological symptoms can be translated into identifiable and concrete difficulties, rather than vague and uncontrollable ones. Such interventions focus upon the individual's beliefs and behaviours rather than on the relationship between the individual's beliefs in the context of his family, and the impact this has on the therapeutic system of professional carers.

Other interventions are described more fully in Box 10.2.

Box 10.2 Skills for managing an impasse in counselling

A number of approaches can be used to break the cycle of 'Yes I am ... No you're not' in counselling. Some of these are powerful interventions and should be used with sensitivity and care. Apparent resistance can be managed as follows:

1. *Comment on the apparent 'stuckness'*
   I feel that each time I try to persuade you that you do not have a tumour, you seem to be quite convinced that you have one. If you were the counsellor in my position, what might you say to a patient?

2. *Adopt a one-down, defeated position*
   (Somewhat theatrically, looking exasperated) Well, well, well; Steve, you seem to have got me here. I just can't think how I'm going to change your ideas. I just don't seem to be able to throw any new light on this. I'll need to think about this for a while.

---

3. *Solicit the patient's help*
   Do you have any ideas about what might help to convince you that you don't have a tumour and and that you are not dying?

4. *Discuss the effect of the worry on relationships*
   How has this worry affected your relationship with your wife?

5. *Ask what might happen if the worry persisted*
   If this worry never went away, what effect may this have on you and how might you cope?

6. *Ask what might happen if things got worse (feared catastrophe)*
   What is the worst thing that could happen to you with this problem?

7. *Ask what might replace this worry*
   If, for some reason, you stopped worrying about dying, is there anything else you might start to worry about?

8. *Talk hypothetically about having the illness*
   You keep trying to convince me that you are terminally ill. You don't believe the doctors when they tell you that all the tests were accurate and reliable. Let's pretend for a few minutes that you are terminally ill. Let's talk about a day in your life as a terminally ill young man. How much of the day would you worry about dying? Who would you talk to about it? What plans would you make? What would you do not associated with your illness? How would this be different from what you are doing now?

9. *Discuss some advantages of worrying (reframe)*
   Has your worry resulted in anything good for you?

10. *Indicate that the patient has control*
    You will know when you are ready to stop worrying about your heart and to be convinced that the test results were correct.

Conclusion

Somatizing and 'worried well' dermatology patients present a unique challenge to health care providers in general, and counsellors in particular. Successful treatment requires close collaboration between all professional carers and innovative therapeutic interventions. Some patients may remain unresponsive to treatment, and the possibility of a consultation with or referral to other mental health specialists (such as a clinical psychologist or psychiatrist) may then need to be considered. We have found that there is also a small group of these patients who, once in counselling, keep producing a worry about symptoms of their health in order to maintain access to and contact with the counsellor. This usually occurs when counselling is coming to an end. In such cases, the worry is a ticket of entry to psychological support systems. Unless the counsellor notes this, the patient will revert to the worry at the end of counselling sessions in order to re-engage the counsellor. It can be of some help in these circumstances to say to the patient: 'I will continue to see you for counselling even when you no longer have these worries.' (Some readers familiar with hypnotic techniques will recognize that this is in itself an intervention.) The main concern behind the patient's symptom is then suggested and other issues can be explored. Counsellors need to be sensitive to the different concerns of patients and the indirect ways in which patients may sometimes express these concerns. The principles of managing resistance have been outlined in this chapter and may be applied to other clinical situations in which an impasse develops.

11

Counselling Children and Parents

Introduction

In this chapter we discuss how counselling can be applied to working with children with dermatological problems and their parents. We begin the chapter by addressing the way that parents who have lived with a dermatological problem may react to the prospect of having a child with the same condition. We also highlight relationship difficulties that might arise within families following the birth of a child with a skin disease. Finally we discuss practical ways that parents and teachers can use to help children to cope with difficult peer group situations such as verbal bullying.

Having a child with a dermatological problem

Parents may be very distressed that their child has been diagnosed with a chronic or acute medical condition, and dermatological problems are no exception. Their concerns may be for the health of the child and the emotional and practical demands on the family. Concerns, in some cases, might centre around being responsible for applying treatments, the potential impact on the bonding in the parent–child relationship and the effect on other siblings. Some conditions may be hereditary, and this may bring on additional stresses for parents. Current tests and treatments for genetically transmitted skin diseases aim to minimize the biological consequences of gene mutations. Antenatal testing might be initiated such as **chorionic villus sampling**, fetoscopy and fetal skin biopsy. Before undertaking prenatal diagnosis with any of these methods however, parents need to be counselled about the possible risks involved in the procedures. A decision as to whether the condition is severe enough to justify the risks of the procedure also needs to be made. Although the doctor may provide parents with information regarding risks, the final decision is up to the couple concerned, who will need to give their informed consent. The couple will also need to consider the possible results of the tests, and the implications for their family life. Counselling can help parents by providing information about choices regarding pregnancy and treatment, and support them in making the difficult decisions that often arise with prenatal testing (see Box 11.1)

Box 11.1 Issues in prenatal testing

Maria and Thomas had been married for two years when Maria found out she was pregnant. The pregnancy came as a shock to both of them since they had decided not to plan a family until their finances were settled. Their situation was further complicated by the fact that Thomas had neurofibromatosis, a neurological disorder that caused the appearance of cyst like lumps on his skin. Although Thomas felt that he had come to terms with his condition, he was uncertain that he could cope with 'handing it down' to one of his children. The couple decided to seek counselling as a means to clarify their feelings and options.

Parents may express feelings of guilt and anxiety and their own experience of living with the condition may affect whether or not they decide to proceed with the pregnancy. Some useful areas which the counsellor can explore with the patient are outlined in Box 11.2.

Box 11.2. Helping couples explore their feelings and options

- Help the parents identify what their knowledge is about the disorder, their view about the chances of the child being affected and what difficulties they feel that they or their child will have coping with it.
- Provide information to parents about the disorder and its implications and examine with them if there is a discrepancy between this and their expectations of what the disease will be like.
- Explore issues of guilt and responsibility with parents and challenge self-defeating thoughts around these issues.
- Help parents clarify their choices and options about treatment or care.

Introducing parents to their child with a congenital skin problem

When a child is born with a visible skin disease, it is not always easy for the parents to come to terms with the fact that their child is 'less then perfect'. Parents are likely to have formed expectations of what their child will look like and the tasks that parenting will entail. These expectations may have to be adapted to account for the child's condition, and parents may experience shock, disappointment or even anger when they first see their newborn baby. It is useful therefore when introducing the child to its parents for the first time that health professionals are sensitive to these issues and take steps to make the introduction of the disfigured baby to its parents as easy as possible. This may include:

- showing a picture of another child with the same condition to the parents before the baby is brought to them so that they can form an idea of what the child will look like
- discussing the child's condition with parents and answering any questions they may have regarding duration, course and treatment
- bringing the baby into the room wrapped in a blanket and allowing parents to 'take their time' in examining what their baby looks like
- explaining and modelling the importance of touch, especially if the parents seem anxious about coming into contact with the skin lesions
- providing parents with important sources of support and information such as specialist charities, health care workers and support groups for parents of children with the same condition.

Skin disease and babies

The diagnosis of a progressive or episodic skin condition within the family can be stressful for both the child and parents (Dungey and Busselmeir, 1982). Skin diseases may signal a loss of 'normality', alter the family's concept of its 'self', challenge coping methods and lead to changes in roles, plans and dreams. Parents may blame themselves if they believe the disease to be hereditary and siblings may themselves fear acquiring the disease. Janice is a mother of a 15–month-old baby with eczema and she describes her feelings about her baby in Box 11.3.

Box 11.3 Parental reactions to a child with skin disease

'When Jessica was born, I was really excited that I'd had a little girl. I wanted a girl so much that I had even bought little dresses

---

for her before she was born! She was going to be my little doll. I think when the eczema came on it was a real shock to me. I had heard about the condition but didn't know much about it. I didn't expect that I would have to make so many changes to deal with it. You see, Jessica's skin gets very itchy so she becomes really uncomfortable and cries a lot, and sometimes all through the night. I can't dress her in the clothes that I want because she has a bad reaction to certain fabrics. Also, I have to apply this special ointment to her patches, but she hates that and starts screaming when she sees me coming with the tub of cream. I feel really bad when she struggles with me like that. Sometimes I feel that we aren't close enough, you know. I can't play with her or cuddle her, because she gets really uncomfortable. It's very hard for us. It's like the eczema won't allow me to have the relationship, the closeness that I want with my daughter.'

This case illustrates some of the difficulties that can arise when a young child develops a skin condition. A central concern of this mother was that of her relationship and attachment to her child. Her story illustrates how anxiety provoking it can be not to bond easily with her child. A counsellor might help in such a case by examining ways where touch can be 'de-medicalized' and re-introduced in a positive way into the child–parent relationship. This might be done, for example, at bath time, as this is sometimes soothing for the child's skin, or through the use of playing with textured toys that feel comfortable to the baby. It might also be a good idea that different family members share the responsibility of applying medications or ointments so that the child does not associate the discomfort with only one particular person.

Skin disease and the parent–child relationship

The relationship between the child and the parent may have implications for the way in which the child makes sense of and copes with his or her condition. Research suggests that one of the most significant factors in the development of behavioural problems of children with disfiguring skin conditions is the reaction of the parents to the illness or deformity (Barden, 1990). Over-protective parents who shield their child from social ridicule may prevent the development of peer relationships and social skills, which are vital for later developmental tasks. In a study which examined the response of black South African mothers to the birth of an albino infant (Kromberg et al., 1987), mothers were initially found to be depressed and uncomfortable with close contact with their child and were reluctant to hold and breast feed them. They displayed fewer fondling and touching behaviours in comparison to a matched control group. The feelings of unhappiness and depression regarding the appearance of the child persisted, in most cases, until the infants reached nine months of age. The birth of an infant of a remarkable appearance appeared to cause delay in maternal attachment and resulted in sadness similar to that experienced by mothers of infants with other congenital disorders.

Common reactions of parents which tend to occur with the birth of a child with a skin condition include:

1. *Parental mourning, i.e. the denial, anger and sadness that the parent feels following the birth of the child.* Being informed that one's child is ill or has some handicap is a life crisis which brings with it changes. Parents face the prospect of having to adapt to circumstances that they might not have ever imagined having to contend with. They may go through a mourning period similar to that following the death of a friend or family member.

2. *Disappointment, shame or guilt.* Guilt is a common feeling that accompanies the birth of a child with an illness. This is especially relevant in cases where the illness has been genetically transmitted, but can also occur when the onset cannot be linked to a genetic causes. Parents may have an unrealistic expectation of how the illness will affect the child's life. They may also feel unprepared emotionally, financially and practically to deal with the challenges of bringing up the child. This may make them feel inadequate and add to the feelings of guilt that they have about the child's illness.

3. *Overprotection or over-indulgence stemming from parental anxiety.* The anxiety that parents feel about their child's condition may affect the way that they behave towards them. Parents may become over-protective of their children in order to buffer them against the social and physical consequences of their illness. Similarly they may try to over-compensate for the fact that their child has to live with a chronic skin condition by over-indulgence, causing resentment in other siblings.

4. *Focusing on the needs of the sick child and disregarding or downplaying the needs of the other children in the family.* One of the difficulties that often faces a family that has a child with a chronic skin disease is the way that the illness affects the family as a whole, and how the individual members are affected. In some cases, a parent's guilt regarding the child's illness and need to compensate for it is expressed through an over-involvement with the child. This will inevitably have implications on how the parent will deal with the other children.

5. *Parental neglect or rejection of the sick child.* Another possible parental reaction is one where the child is rejected because the parents do not feel that they can cope with the child's illness. This may stem from the fear that if they get too close emotionally that it will be too dis-

tressing for them. It may also be due to a belief that they will be letting down their child if they are unable to help them cope. Parental rejection can also occur when the disfigurement or skin disease is believed to have resulted from sin or wrong-doing.

6. *Anger or resentment about the financial and practical burdens of care-taking and medical treatment.* Like any illness, skin disease brings with it practical challenges with which the family will have to contend. Depending on the condition, parents may have to make changes to their daily routine, such as taking the child to the clinic or treatment centre. The issue of cost may also arise where parents have to find ways of financing either treatment or care-taking of their child because of their illness. All these factors may contribute to making parents feel resentful of the amount of time and effort that they have to put into the management of their child's condition.

7. *Parental depression and fatigue.* The factors described above can lead to depression and fatigue in parents. In cases where the child's condition is chronic or episodic, the parents may feel that they have no control over the child's illness and that their efforts to improve the child's condition are in vain. The fact that so much of their energy is centred on the child and the illness means that their own needs are likely to go unmet and that fatigue and depression are likely to occur.

8. *Marital problems between parents.* Illness resonates throughout the whole family and relationships between family members can often be adversely affected. Parents of an ill child may become so absorbed with their child's condition that they begin to neglect their own needs and those of other family members. They may find it difficult to share their feelings with others and can therefore isolate themselves from their partner and other family members.

Factors that affect adaptation to skin disease in children

It has been suggested that the clinical manifestations of skin conditions in children such as psoriasis are affected by two factors: the degree of adaptiveness and the level of anxiety (Kerr, 1992). Although anxiety may be experienced by individuals, it is also a property of the family system. To some extent, the way in which family members relate to each other is responsible for generating chronic anxiety. Therefore, the higher the levels of anxiety in the family system, the greater the strain put upon each individual's adaptive capacity. The more adaptive family members are, the easier it becomes for one person to become anxious without evoking anxiety from other family members. This way of relating allows family members to become supportively involved rather than withdrawing or becoming anxiously focused on each other. If this degree of differentiation is maintained, the family system will be able to successfully adapt to the possibility of future disruptive events or changes.

Although the visibility and severity of the skin condition may have an effect on how well a child adapts to the illness, there is not necessarily a direct relationship between the two. As in the case of adults, a range of other factors are predictors of how a child will cope with the condition. Children who have strong social support, a supportive family environment and psychological resources, such as high levels of self-esteem and creativity, are less likely to be negatively affected by their condition than those children who do not have these resources. The psychological and emotional well being of children with dermatological problems therefore, does not depend on their physical status but rather on differences in family functioning, social support and religious or philosophical attitudes (Beuf, 1990) (see Figure 11.1).

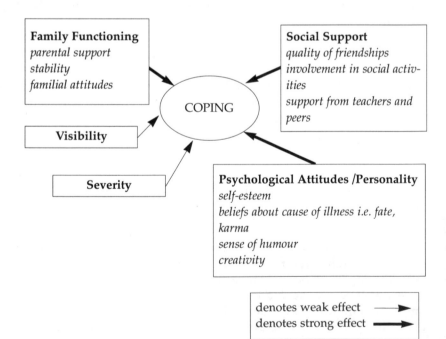

Figure 11.1: Influences on children's coping

Coping with teasing

Apart from the child's family, the school environment is likely to be the next most important context which affects a child's adjustment. Children who are obviously visibly different from their peers may attract negative attention leading to teasing and bullying. These actions may in turn affect the social and interpersonal skills that the child develops, and in some cases can even interfere with learning. Although some children are able to confide in their parents about experiences of having been teased or bullied, others may feel unable to tell anyone about how they feel. Some indications that a child may be being bullied at school include: reluctance to attend school; reluctance to go out and play; showing signs of low mood such as being less talkative, appearing troubled or sad; and displaying disruptive behaviour.

When it has been established that a child is being bullied, this needs to be taken seriously by both parents and teachers, and immediate action should be taken by them. This may mean that parents need to meet with the child's teacher to discuss their concerns and find ways of dealing with the problem. Some schools have well-defined procedures in place to deal with bullying and teasing. It is important that parents are informed about how the school intends to deal with the problem and the effectiveness of any action taken. Children who are bullied need to be made aware that it is not their 'fault' that they are being teased. This may encourage them to discuss their problems with parents, teachers or even friends, rather then feeling isolated and attempting to cope on their own. Children should also be encouraged to recognize that they have some control over the situation and that they can rely on the support of adults in these situations. Parents can help by discussing with the child how he or she might deal with rude comments or teasing, and teach the child to assert themselves in a non-aggressive way (see the case in Box 11.4).

Box 11.4 Coping with bullying

Jasper moved down to London with his parents from a rural village where he was born when he was nine years old. Until then he had been a happy child and although he had a large port wine stain on the left side of his face and neck, this had never caused any significant problem for him. The people in his village knew Jasper and his family well, and since it was a small community he only rarely came into contact with strangers. Jasper's mother, Susan, was concerned about how he would settle in his new school and whether the port-wine stain would create any

---

problems for him. She discussed this with her son who assured her that it wouldn't be a problem for him. Jasper started his new school in September and his mother recalls his first day as being relatively uneventful. Jasper had come home and explained that he had met his new teacher and classmates, whomm he seemed to like, and that his birthmark had not been a problem. As the weeks progressed however, Susan began to notice that Jasper was becoming more and more withdrawn. He spent long hours alone in his room and no longer enjoyed riding his bike or playing in the garden. When Susan tried to ask him if everything was all right at school, he would become agitated and say that things were 'fine' and that she should leave him alone. In early November, Susan decided to contact the school and discuss her concerns. The teacher indicated that he was not participating in class and had also noticed that he spent breaks and lunch times by himself. She indicated that there was one incident where one of the children had put red paint on his cheek during art class, and shouted out that he was Jasper. The teacher said that the child had been 'told off' and that she thought that since then, no one else had made an issue of it. The teacher also explained that she thought that Jasper was a shy child by nature and that since he was new at the school, that he appeared shy and withdrawn did not seem strange. Susan indicated to the teacher that Jasper had never been a shy child and expressed her concerns about bullying. Over the next few weeks, Susan had several meetings with Jasper's teacher and the other teaching staff to decide how to tackle the problem. First, they agreed that there would be more of an effort during class to reward children for pro-social behaviour such as being thoughtful and courteous to one another. It was also agreed that more emphasis would be placed on collaboration and group projects, thereby providing an environment where the children had to work together towards a common goal. Through this, ability rather than appearance would be emphasized and valued and Jasper would be given the opportunity to form closer bonds with his peers. It was also suggested that Jasper be asked whether he wanted to talk to his classmates about why he looked the way he did, since much of the problem centred around the children's curiosity about Jasper's appearance. Susan was not convinced about this last suggestion and said that she would discuss it with her son. Finally, Susan and Jasper's teacher decided to remain in close contact and inform each other of Jasper's progress without his having to face the whole class and thereby singling him out.

At home, Susan decided to try and tackle the problem with Jasper. She first tried to work on his self-esteem by helping him to externalize the children's reactions. She explained to him that the rudeness of some of his peers said a lot more about them then it did about him. She also explained that some of the children were probably ignorant about why he had his mark and what it felt like and may have been reacting the way they were out of curiosity. They talked about how he could use humour to deal with awkward situations and explained how important it was to remember that he should not feel that he should have to change who he was or what he liked to do because of other people. They also agreed that they would talk to each other when they were having a hard time or felt sad when they were missing friends from their old village. Over the next few months, Jasper became more involved with school, spent less time alone in his room and established a friendship with a girl in his class. Although from time to time he still experienced some rude and hurtful reactions, he felt more confident in himself and had greater support from those around him

Explaining skin disease to other children

The above case illustrates a mother's concern about how her son may be teased because of his skin condition. Children's questions about skin problems and disfigurement can often seem intrusive and difficult to answer. Children as young as three years have shown a preference for choosing attractive peers for friends (Conant and Budoff, 1983) and children with even minor facial anomalies are often stigmatized by their peers (Sigelman et al., 1986). In some cases, explaining to a child the causes and effects of certain conditions may dispel certain fears or fantasies that they have about a particular disease (Partridge, 1994). Helping children 'get over' their curiosity about a condition can help them to focus on other aspects of the child not necessarily related to their appearance (See Box 11.5).

Box 11. 5 *Explaining skin disease to children*

Samantha was a happy outgoing 6-year-old who had been born with a large port-wine stain on the left side of her face and neck. The mark did not seem to bother Samantha. She and her mother referred to it as her 'strawberry stamp', and joked about how it was proof that she loved strawberry ice-cream. When she was around other children, they would ask her questions about it and she seemed comfortable talking about it and consequently did not appear to have difficulties engaging with other children. As the time approached when she would be starting school, her mother, Janice, began to feel concerned about how other children in the class would react to her. She decided to speak to a teacher at the school who suggested that it might be a good idea if Samantha could talk to them about her birthmark. She suggested that through this any erroneous ideas that the other children had about Samantha could be dispelled and she could take control of the situation by offering explanations that she felt comfortable and happy with. Janice discussed the teacher's suggestion with her daughter who seemed quite excited about the idea of talking to the other children about her 'strawberry stamp'. Samantha was able to talk about her mark and give a description of how it made her feel, how it didn't hurt to touch and about how much she really liked eating strawberry ice-cream and that she and her mother often joked that it showed! The other children reacted positively towards Samantha; with their curiosity satisfied at an early stage and any fears they had dispelled, Samantha was able to settle into her new class and the issue of her 'strawberry stamp' rarely came up with her friends or classmates.

Adolescence

With the onset of puberty, the need to feel closely connected and accepted by one's peers is strong. Being part of a group makes us feel supported and allows us to define an identity outside our family and home life. Children who are somehow different either through their appearance or through illness may have this sense of belonging challenged. Some of these children may begin to internalize negative comments and experiences from social encounters during puberty, even though they may have appeared to cope well during childhood (Lefebvre et al., 1986). In cases such as these, living with a skin condition can be especially difficult. Hopes of forming new relationships and establishing sexual relationships may be erased for fear of rejection. Similarly, school and career prospects may be adversely affected and tailored to suit the low self-concept of the individual. Of course adolescence is also a time when acne may first develop. This can be a source of a great deal of distress for the affected person. Anecdotal reports suggest that a proportion of teenage suicides result from concerns about body image. Comments such as 'pizza face' and 'pimple farm' may be heard in the classroom and may cause distress to the individual who in turn may become withdrawn, depressed or act truant from school. Teachers and parents need to be aware of this and should be sensitive to the prospect of bullying and the reasons for poor school performance.

Acne may also appear at a time when the adolescent experiences other physical and emotional changes resulting from growth and hormonal activity. These may exacerbate emotional reactions leading some parents, teachers and even peers to try to reassure the adolescent through telling him or her that it is something not to worry about. Evidence suggests that some adolescents feel too self-conscious even to share with their GP or school counsellor their feelings of distress. For this reason the school and parents should be more proactive and openly discuss the topic in a general way, alongside other topics that affect adolescence, such as sex, relationships and drugs, rather than waiting for specific problems to come to their attention. The counselling skills described in this book are equally applicable to working with adolescents with skin problems.

Psychological distress associated with acne and other skin complaints should not be trivialized or overlooked with this group. The fact is that through the use of modern treatments acne can be controlled and cured. However, counsellors and other health care professionals should keep in mind that there have been reports of clinical depression and even suicide in a small number of patients (particularly adolescents) who were being treated with the more powerful anti-acne medications. It is unclear however, whether this is directly caused by treatment, a co-factor or the result of low mood due to stigma resulting from their skin condition.

We end this chapter with a quotation in Box 11.6 from a 16–year-old boy with severe acne which captures the profound effect it has on adolescents.

Box 11.6

'Other lads my age dream of winning the lottery or playing for Man. United. All I ever wish for is that my face will be normal again, that I'll be able to look in the mirror without cringing, that I'll be able to walk down the street and look people in the eye. I know that it sounds stupid, but sometimes I see people in wheelchairs and I think "well they're luckier than me, at least they have good skin". You see, my skin is the last thing that I think about when I go to bed at night and the first thing that I think about when I wake up in the morning, it's always on my mind.'

Conclusion

In this chapter we have highlighted some of the issues that evolve during childhood with regard to skin disease. The importance of genetic counselling has been considered and suggestions given as to how counselling can help patients prior to the birth of their child. Parental reactions to a birth of a child with a disfiguring skin condition can affect how the child copes with the condition. Furthermore, the family itself may be affected by the child's condition, with parents and siblings having to contend with added responsibilities and cope with their own reaction to the disease. Skin disease often raises different challenges for the child at different ages. Issues such as teasing may be more of an issue in younger years, whereas those pertaining to group involvement and relationships may be more salient as the child grows up. The period of adolescence and increasing feelings of self-consciousness and the appearance of acne can be problematic and often require sensible professional help.

12

Working in a Multidisciplinary Team

Introduction

Having addressed the psychosocial problems that may arise with people affected by a skin condition, and illustrated how counselling can be used in dermatology settings, we now turn our attention to the issue of working in multidisciplinary teams. Because most skin problems are not life-threatening, dermatology is predominantly an outpatient specialty, although skin specialists also consult with inpatients, particularly but not only if the patient's dermatological problem is secondary to another medical problem (e.g. HIV or liver disease), iatrogenic (a reaction to a prescribed medication or treatment), perhaps stress-related or even induced by the patient himself. The multidisciplinary teams caring for dermatology patients, however, tend to be smaller than those in other specialties such as neurosurgery, haematology and paediatrics. Nevertheless, increasing recognition of the psychological needs of patients, as well as of issues relating to treatment compliance, have recently led to expansion of the multidisciplinary dermatology team in some settings. Such teams comprise consultants, junior doctors, nurses, district nurses, camouflage specialists, psychologists and counsellors, among others. Effective collaboration between all these professionals is an acquired skill and essential if patients are to benefit fully from the specialist team.

Counsellors working in dermatology settings

The presence of a counsellor within the dermatology setting is a recent development, and by no means without its complications. From the counsellor's perspective, numerous contextual issues must first be addressed before embarking on a course of sessions with a patient. Clarification from referrers and other colleagues about the role and position of the counsellor in a specific case is an important first step.

Failure to attend to relationships with the referrer or with other health care professionals, not only at the start of the counselling service, but throughout the duration of the service, could undermine the service and even lead to its termination.

Some counsellors believe that counselling can help in all areas of patient care and management. However, such confidence expressed openly could thwart counsellors' integration into these health care teams. In most health care settings, counselling is secondary to medical and nursing care, however important and pressing the psychological and social components implications of an illness may be. The challenge for counsellors is to find a way into the team without posing a threat to colleagues. This chapter describes how different professional collaborations and consultations in dermatology clinics can facilitate a wider range of interesting and creative ways of working with colleagues and patients, thereby enabling counsellors to have a secure place in the team.

The entry of the counsellor into the dermatology team is potentially complex and may be time-consuming. However, the need for a counselling service may arise for a number of reasons, such as:

- increasing workloads and administrative demands may make it difficult for doctors and nurses to address all of the patient's psychological needs, which may be complex and time-consuming;
- some members of a team may have experience of or have heard about the usefulness of having a counsellor as part of their team;
- a suggestion may be made by a counsellor that a dermatology service could benefit from having a counsellor to help solve and manage some of their patients' problems;
- an element of competitiveness may mean that staff pay 'lip service' to the idea of having a counsellor just because other medical teams are doing it;
- the team may experience benefit from referral to a counsellor and invite him or her to join them.

How a counselling service is introduced and developed will also depend on whether there are existing protocols for psychosocial care. The counsellor should thus adopt a non-oppositional stance, irrespective of whether the environment is receptive, cautious or hostile. Such a stance can help the counsellor integrate into the team and gain acceptance from colleagues. This entails having small goals, starting by learning about the unit, building up credit with one's colleagues and avoiding criticism. Attitudes of hostility or caution may stem from myths or stereotypes about each professional group, either due to past experience or as a defence against the introduction of something different or new. Counsellors and health care professionals sometimes have stereotypic views of one another (McDaniel and Campbell, 1986).

Doctors' and nurses' myths about counsellors:

- providers of 'tea and sympathy' or a shoulder to cry on
- 'do-gooders' who try to cheer people up
- not properly trained, or unprofessional amateurs
- overly sensitive
- what they do with patients is plain common sense
- glorified agony aunts offering a listening service
- a last resort with difficult patients
- time wasters who sit and talk
- useful only for dealing with hypochondriacs and panic attacks
- outcome or effectiveness cannot be measured
- they analyse too much

Counsellors' myths about doctors and nurses

- preoccupied with the boundaries and limits of their own competence
- unable to share easily
- not open to new ideas
- offer only hi-tech and impersonal care
- bedside manner is superficial
- territorial and do not work easily with new colleagues
- medical model of practice is vastly different to the counselling model
- assume power and act in a patronizing manner
- use props (white coats, stethoscopes, beepers) to identify themselves and create distance
- stressed, and some could do with counselling for themselves
- believe that they already do limited counselling with their patients

Some of these ideas may, at first, seem amusing or even ludicrous. The fact is that however amicably members of some multiprofessional health care teams get on with one another, they may approach and deliver patient care differently and hold constraining and sometimes erroneous beliefs about one another. An awareness may help counsellors practise in such a way as not to conform to these stereotypes and avoid being defensive or oppositional when they are voiced. This will go a long way to building up collaborative working relationships with colleagues. The context or setting in which the counsellor works also affects the range of possible collaborative relationships that can be fostered.

Below is a list of hints which may facilitate the counsellor's integration into the mutidicplinary dermatology team.

Practical hints for improving collaboration in health care settings

The ideas below are mostly applicable to counsellors who work or wish to work as part of a multidisciplinary team, although some points may have relevance to other professionals.

- Make no assumptions about what constitutes a problem, for whom it is a problem, how people should cope with illness, disfigurement or disability, or how they should relate to one another. Also, do not assume that they understand their illness, its implications, treatment and so on.
- Practise collaboratively as a part of a team; dispel the myth that counsellors always have their own agenda and 'get on their high horse' in order to assert their views and opinions.
- Be humble but communicate directly. Learn from others and be tentative if you are unsure. Do not overstate the importance of counselling – patients rarely live or die by what happens in counselling, and medical and nursing concerns should take precedence. Refer patients to other colleagues where appropriate, but do not be reticent to offer directives if indicated.
- Learn about health care issues by attending case meetings and lectures, sitting in with doctors when they consult with patients, learning the language of the health care staff and acquiring and developing an interest in anthropology and sociology so as to learn more about the health care setting.
- Be curious; adopt a stance of receptive openness and ask questions. Avoid making assumptions and becoming prescriptive.
- Be flexible about where you see patients and when you see them, your working hours, the approaches used in counselling for which there may be special demands in a health care setting (cognitive-behavioural and family therapy); work at the patient's pace and determine whether the problem is best solved by open-ended, exploratory counselling or by problem-focused counselling.
- Be time conscious; aim to achieve the most within the time constraints. Learn how to do counselling briefly. When feeding back to other colleagues either verbally or in a letter, be succinct and to the point; avoid wordy and lengthy reports, and unfocused discussions about patients.
- Be proactive by not waiting for problems to occur or for patients to start discussing their main concerns and fears. Waiting for patients to talk about these may be too late to help in any practical way as the patient may believe that you too are colluding with his denial of the problem.
- Where appropriate, give information; counselling should be more a

dialogue than a monologue. Do not be afraid to give advice or suggest to whom a patient can talk if he or she requires more specialist information (although doctors and nurses must be consulted).

- Practise defensively; patients are increasingly conscious of their rights and what they can expect from health care professionals in the course of their treatment. In some cases this can lead to litigation or complaints to hospital/clinic managers or your professional body. The likelihood of this is reduced if (a) you refrain from making unrealistic claims, (b) you defer to doctors or nurses when in doubt about how to deal with a problem, (c) you keep factual notes of what happens in sessions but limit your opinions to what has been deduced from observations of behaviour, i.e. have evidence, and, (d) by being curious and only offering ideas and opinions tentatively. Be accountable to your profession, colleagues and managers of the institution or setting in which you practise by giving feedback about your work and related problems without necessarily breaching patient confidentiality.
- Be practical; as counsellors we are sometimes longwinded and overly cerebral in response to patient problems. Learn to make rapid decisions, to take small risks and think imaginatively, yet practically, about possible solutions.
- Respect patients' defences, which may serve to protect them. Talk about what you observe with the patient, but it is not always necessary to confront or directly challenge their defences. Counter any suggestion of blame for illness from either the patient or family members.
- Sustain realistic hope; therapeutic neutrality sometimes interferes with our ability to offer supportive and comforting words to the patient and others. By focusing on practical issues it may be possible to give a message of some realistic hope without denying the gravity of the situation. Similarly, it is important not to shy away from discussing issues about death, dying, disfigurement, loss and pain when it is obvious that these need to be openly addressed. Help the patient to see a future and to participate in decision-making for the future.
- Help patients to gain a sense of mastery over their situations by involving them in decisions. Work toward increasing their choices or options. Avoid fostering too much dependence as this may be counter-productive.
- Evaluate your practice; it is good practice to audit and evaluate your work. This can also help in the maintenance and development of your counselling service. Decisions about health care delivery are increasingly made on evidence-based practice. Evaluation and audit of counselling practice should be initiated by counsellors ,otherwise there is a danger that others will take charge of the evaluation process.

Definition of problem	Example
1. With patients	A dermatologist asks for advice from a counsellor about how to manage a patient who will not comply with treatment.
2. With patients and relatives	A patient complains to a clinic manager about his treatment and care.
3. With managers	A counsellor is invited to comment on a document drafted by medical colleagues which sets out how patient care can be improved.
4. With colleagues	High staff turnover in a dermatology clinic prompts senior medical and nursing staff to consult with a counsellor to see whether this problem might be caused by staff relationship problems or by how the service is organized and managed.
5. Within a team	A new staff member joins the team. A counsellor is invited to facilitate a team-building event.

Figure 12.1 Problems that prompt requests for consultation

- Dress according to the context. Unlike doctors and nurses, counsellors do not have a uniform or any props (stethoscopes or white coats) which may identify them. Even so, most hospitals and clinics are rather conservative establishments and the expectation is to be dressed in conservative and formal attire. Expectations may be different for counsellors working in community and outreach settings.
- Teach others; the accusation that some counsellors do not help other health care professionals to understand more about psychological process and counselling is not without foundation. Offer to give seminars, invite colleagues to case discussions, collaborate in research and offer to see patients jointly with another professional colleague. Foster a climate of openness about your work, as this may help others to understand better what you do with patients and may lead to them being more supportive of your service.

The counsellor can organize his or her practice in a number of different ways, depending upon the needs of the service and his or her level of competence and experience. This involves direct or indirect patient or colleague consultations, or any combination of these, listed as follows: counsellor practice can include: consultations with patients only; consultations with professional staff only about the care of their patients; consultations with professional staff about staff relationships; consultations with both staff and patients; *ad hoc* consultations with either staff or patients (i.e. consultation-liaison practice).

A well-trained and experienced counsellor need not have an extensive knowledge of a particular dermatological condition, although this helps in gaining the confidence of the team. However, an understanding of the context in which treatment and care is provided is a vital first step. Having a framework for consultation with other health care professionals in health care settings can help to achieve these aims.

Problems or events that typically prompt a request for consultation in health care settings stem from one of five possibilities, even though they may be linked. These are listed in Figure 12.1.

There are many other examples of consultation work and it is important to stress that many of these are only indirectly concerned with patient problems.

Dermatologists' perspectives on counselling

The recent emphasis on addressing the psychological consequences of illnesses and health problems has meant that many physicians have had to consider these matters with regard to their patients' own conditions. In the case of skin disease, this has been to some extent problematic in the past for two reasons:

1. *Most GPs receive only limited training in dermatology.* In many cases the first port of call for a dermatology patient is the GP. However, given the fact that many have not received a specialist training in skin disease, the patient may be misdiagnosed, improperly treated or in many cases dismissed, being told not to worry about it. This is particularly problematic considering that 10–15% of the average GP workload centres around treating skin disease; this could adversely affect the disease outcome or even create or exacerbate a psychological problem related to the skin problem.
2. Dermatology does not have a strong voice in the medical fraternity. Many dermatologists acknowledge the need for more general physician training in skin disease, and also the need for more collaborative care for dermatology patients with psychological problems. However, in the field of medicine, such improvements in patient care may depend more upon seemingly unrelated factors

such as the number of in-patients in a hospital and the mortality rates for particular conditions. Since dermatology is primarily an out-patient specialty, the development of multidisciplinary health care teams for treating people with skin disorders has been relatively slow.

How dermatologists give bad news to patients

As with all medical specialties, dermatologists find themselves having to give bad news to patients from time to time. This may not necessarily be in the form of a death sentence, but rather news of limited treatment options associated with an illness. If handled properly, however, the giving of bad or unwelcome news can facilitate patient coping and adaptation to their condition. Below we outline some ideas that can help doctors in dealing with giving bad news to patients.

Dermatologists should:

- adopt an optimistic approach towards the patient, explaining the difficulties but also highlighting any possible alternatives that may exist regarding treatment and care;
- give the patient time to think about and digest what has been said. Perhaps a follow-up appointment might be made where patients can come and discuss issues that they were unable to address because of shock or anxiety when they were initially told about their condition;
- discuss any questions and concerns patients may have about their condition, and allay any myths or erroneous views they may hold regarding the course, duration and cause of the condition;
- realize that patients' beliefs should be central to the discussion, and not make assumptions about the psychological effects the condition will have on the patient;
- be aware of cultural differences: different skin conditions may for example be more distressing than others depending on the cultural stigma associated with them.

How care can inadvertently harm patients

In some cases, even when the dermatologist has sympathetically given the patient bad news and counselled him or her, some patients might be so desperate to hear that their condition is treatable that they will often seek alternative therapies as a means of treatment. Although some of these might conceivably have some beneficial effects, in most cases they will be ineffective and even make the patient more depressed and upset about their condition (see box 12.1).

Box 12.1 Dubious alternative treatments: the case of a psoriasis patient

A psoriasis patient recently gave an account of his experience with a person who was offering a cure for the condition. He explained that he had obtained the number of the 'doctor' from the back of a magazine where 'once and for all cures' for a variety of skin conditions, had been advertised. When he attended the clinic, a man in a white coat examined him and gave him a jar of white cream which he was told to put all over his body twice a day. He was charged an excessive amount for the cream, which he used for six months, but to no avail. He became depressed and when he confronted the so-called doctor he was informed that he had never been promised a cure, and that he should stop being so emotional!

Cases such as these abound and it is important that doctors are aware of the vulnerability of certain patients to seek out alternative, unconfirmed treatments, and perhaps make an effort beforehand to anticipate this and discuss the implications with them.

Conclusion

Consultation skills make it possible for counsellors to relate collaboratively and effectively to their professional colleagues. They also pave the way for developing collaborative work with colleagues. Where joint consultation sessions are held with patients, doctors and nurses, counsellors also learn more about counselling skills and techniques, and counsellors acquire a better understanding of dermatology and health care issues. In turn, patients benefit from better co-ordinated care. This chapter has described how the counsellor can organize his or her work with both professional colleagues and with patients. However elaborate or interesting the counsellor's ideas and interventions might be, they will be marginalized and ultimately rejected by colleagues if they do not strive to work collaboratively. This may be especially challenging for the counsellor who appropriately preserves the confidential nature of sessions with patients, but is also regarded as a team member and is expected to interact with professional colleagues. Counsellors should further seek to arrange professional supervision and support in order to enhance their practice and skills, as well as to reflect the dilemmas and problems that may arise from working within a multidisciplinary team and with people and their families who are affected by illness and health problems.

Many issues have been addressed and questions answered in this book. However, a theme that has been repeatedly highlighted is that the effects of skin disease are more than skin deep. In a world where so much importance is placed on physical appearance, it is increasingly likely that people will be adversely affected by the social and psychological consequences of any stigmatizing condition. As health professionals, we have a duty to understand the illness experience of our patients and seek to explore new methods and treatments for giving them the best care possible.

References

Adler, A. (1907). *Inferiority of Organs*. As cited in Whitlock, F.A. (1976). *Psychophysiological Aspects of Skin Disease*. London: W.B Saunders Limited.

Al'Abadie, M.S.K., Kent, G.G. and Gawkrodger, D.J. (1994). The relationship between stress and the onset and exacerbation of psoriasis and other skin conditions. *British Journal of Dermatology, 130*: 199–203.

Alexander, F. (1950). *Psychosomatic Medicine: Its Principles and Practice*. New York: Norton.

Alexander, F., French, T.M. and Pollock, G.H. (eds). (1968). *Psychosomatic Specificity*. Chicago: University of Chicago Press.

Baker, C., (1992). Factors associated with rehabilitation in head and neck cancer. *Cancer Nursing, 5*: 395–400.

Barber, T.X. (1978). Hypnosis, suggestions and psychosomatic phenomena: a new look from the standpoint of recent experimental studies. *American Journal of Clinical Hypnosis*, 21:13–27.

Barden, R.C. (1990). Clinical management of the cleft lip/palate patient. In M. Green and R. J. Haggarty (eds), *Ambulatory Pediatrics* (5th ed.). New York: Harcourt Brace Jovanovich.

Beard, G.M. (1880). *A Practical Treatise on Nervous Exhaustion*. As cited in Whitlock, F.A. (1976). *Psychophysiological Aspects of Skin Disease*. London: W.B. Saunders Limited.

Beck, A. (1976). *Cognitive Therapy and Emotional Disorders*. New York: International Universities Press.

Behere, P.B. (1981). Psychological reactions to leprosy. *Leprosy in India, 53*(2): 266–272.

Behl, P.N. and Kapoor, T.R. (1995). A clinico-etiological study of 2000 fresh vitiligo patients. *Asian Clinics in Dermatology, 1*(1): 29–33.

Bethune, H.C and Kidd, C.B. (1961). Psychophysiological mechanisms in skin disease. *Lancet, 2*: 1419.

Beuf, A.H. (1990). *Beauty is the Beast: Appearance Impaired Children in America*. Philadelphia: University of Pennsylvania Press.

Blakeney, P., Herndon, D., Desai, M., et al. (1988). Long term psychosocial adjustment following burn injury. *Journal of Burn Care and Rehabilitation, 9*: 661–665.

Bondi, E.E., Jegasothy, B.V. and Lazarus, G. (1991). *Dermatology: Diagnosis and Therapy*. London: Prentice-Hall.

Bor, R., Miller, R., Latz, M. and Salt, H. (1998) *Counselling in Health Care Settings*. London: Cassell.

Bowlby, J. (1975). *The Making and Breaking of Affectional Bonds*. London: Tavistock.

Bradbury, E. (1996). *Counselling People with Disfigurement*. Leicester: BPS Books (British Psychological Society).

Bridgett, C.K. (1996). *Atopic Skin Disease*. Petersfield: Wrightson.

Brown, B., Roberts, J. and Browne, G. (1988). Gender differences in variables associated with psychosocial adjustment to a burn injury. *Nursing and Health*, *11*: 23–30.

Brown, D.G and Bettley, F.R. (1971). Psychiatric treatment of eczema: a controlled trial. *British Medical Journal*, 2: 729–734.

Brown, D.G., and Fromm, D., (1987).). As cited in Sheridan, C.L. and Radmacher, S.A. (1991). *Health Psychology: Challenging the Biomedical Model*. New York: John Wiley and Sons.

Bukley, L.D. (1906). Relations of disease of the skin to internal disorders. As cited in Whitlock, F.A. (1976). *Psychophysiological Aspects of Skin Disease*. London: W.B Saunders Limited.

Byng-Hall, J. (1995). *Rewriting Family Scripts*. New York: Guilford Press.

Carter, B. and McGoldrick, M. (1981). The Family Life Cycle. New York: Gardiner Press.

Cash, T. F. (1990). *The Body Image Automatic Thoughts Questionnaire (BIATQ)*. Norfolk: Department of Psychology, Old Dominion University.

Cash, T.F., and Pruzinsky, T. (1990). *Body Images: Development, Deviance and Change*. New York : Guilford Publications Inc.

Cash, T.F. Winstead, B.W and Janda, L.H. (1986). The great American shape up: body image survey report. *Psychology Today*, *20*: 30–37.

Cole, C.C., Roth, H.L. and Sachs, L.B. (1988). Group psychotherapy as an aid in the medical treatment of eczema. *Journal of the American Academy of Dermatology*, *18*: 286–289.

Conat, S. and Budof, M. (1983). Patterns of awareness of children's understanding of disabilities. *Mental Retardation*, *21*: 119–125.

Dungey, R.K. and Buselmeir, T.J. (1982). Medical and psychosocial aspects of psoriasis. *Health and Social Work*, 140-147.

Edwards, M. and Davis, H. (1998). *Counselling Children with Chronic Medical Conditions*. Leicester: BPS Books.

Engel, G.L., (1977). The need for a new medical model: a challenge for biomedicine. *Science*, *196*: 129–136.

Field, T., and Vega-Lahr, N. (1984). Early interactions between infants with carniofacial anomalies and their mothers. *Infant Behaviour and Development*, 7: 527–530.

Finlay, A.Y., and Khan., G.K., (1992). *The Dermatology Life Quality Index (DLQI.)* Cardiff: University of Wales, College of Medicine.

Frankel, F.H. and Misch, R.C. (1973) Psoriasis and hypnosis. *International Journal of Clinical Psychotherapy and Psychosomatics*, *21*: 121–123.

Gawkrodger, D.A. (1997). *Dermatology: An Illustrated Colour Text*. New York: Churchill Livingstone.

Gill, K.M., Keefe, F.J., Sampson, H.A., McCaskill, C.C., Rodin, J., and Crisson, J.E. (1987) The relationship of stress and family environment to atopic dermatitis symptoms in children. *Journal of Psychosomatic Research*, *31*(6): 673–684.

Ginsburg, I.H. and Link, B.G. (1989). Feelings of stigmatization in patients with psoriasis. *Journal of the American Academy of Dermatology*, *261*(3): 418–419.

Ginsburg, I.H., Prystowsky, J.H., Kornfeld, D.S., and Wolland, H. (1993). Role of emotional factors in adults with atopic dermatitis. *International Journal of Dermatology*, *32*: 656–660.

Gray, S.G. and Lawlis, G.F., (1982). A case study of pruritic eczema treated by relaxation and imagery. *Psychological Reports, 51* (2): 627–633.

Greismer, R.D. (1978). Emotionally triggered disease in dermatological practice. *Psychiatric Annals, 8*: 49–56.

Gupta, M.A., Gupta, A.K. and Haberman, H.F. (1987). The self inflicted dermatoses: a critical review. *General Hospital Psychiatry, 9*: 45–52.

Gupta, M.A. and Vorhees, J.J. (1990). Psychosomatic dermatology. *Archives of Dermatology, 126*: 90–93.

Hall, H.R. (1982). Hypnosis and the immune system: a review with implications for cancer and the psychology of healing. *American Journal of Clinical Hypnosis, 25*: 92–103.

Hawton, K., Salkovskis, P.M., Kirk, J. and Clark, D.M. (1994). *Cognitive Behaviour Therapy for Psychiatric Problems: A Practical Guide.* Oxford : Oxford University Press.

Heindrickz, B., Van Mooffaert, M., Spiers, R. and Von Frenckell, J.R. (1991). The treatment of psychocutaneous disorder: a new approach. *Current Therapeutic Research. 49*(1): 111–119.

Hillier, F. (1865). As in Whitlock, F.A. (1976). *Psychophysiological Aspects of Skin Disease.* London: W.B Saunders Limited.

Horne, D.J. De L., White, A.E., Varigos, G.A. (1989). A preliminary study of psychological therapy in the study of atopic dermatitis. *British Journal of Medical Psychology. 62*: 241–248.

Hughes, J.E., Barraclough, B.M., Hamblin, L.G. and White, J.E. (1983). Psychiatric symptoms in dermatology patients. *British Journal of Psychiatry, 143*: 51–54.

Jachuck, S.J., Brierly, H., Jachuck, S., and Wilcox, P.M. (1982). The effect of hypotensive drugs on the quality of life. *Journal of the Royal College of General Practitioners. 32*: 103–105.

Jowett, S. and Ryan, T. (1985). Skin disease and handicap: an analysis of the impact of skin conditions. *Social Science and Medicine, 20*(4): 425–429.

Kelly, G. (1969). Man's construction of his alternatives. In B. Maher (ed.) *Clinical Psychology and Personality: The Selected Papers of George Kelly.* New York: John Wiley.

Kent, G. and Al'Abadie, M.S.K. (1996). Factors affecting responses on dermatology life quality index items among vitiligo sufferers. *Clinical and Experimental Dermatology, 21*: 330–333.

Kerr, M.E. (1992). Physical illness and the family emotional system: psoriasis as model. *Behavioural Medicine, 18*: 101–113.

Kleber, R.J., and Brom, D. (1992). *Coping with Trauma: Theory, Prevention and Treatment.* Amsterdam: Swets and Zeitlinger.

Kleinman, A., (1988). *The Illness Narratives: Suffering, Healing and the Human Condition.* New York: Basic Books.

Kromberg, J., Zwane, E.M., Jenkins, T., (1987). The response of black mothers to the birth of an albino infant. *American Journal of Diseases of Children, 141*: 911–916.

Lanigan, S., and Cottteril, J. (1989). Psychological disabilities amongst patients with port wine stains. *British Journal of Dermatology, 121*, 209–215.

Lansdown, R.L., Rumsey, N., Bradbury, E., Carr, T. and Partridge, J. (1997) *Visibly Different: Coping with Disfigurement.* Oxford: Butterworth Heinemann.

Lazarus, R.S. (1993). Coping theory and research: past, present and future. *Psychosomatic Medicine, 55*: 243–247.

Lazarus, R.S. and Folkman, S. (1984). *Stress, Appraisal and Coping.* New York: Springer.

Le Poole, I.C., Das, P.K, and van der Wijngaard, R.M.J.G.J. et al., (1993). Review of the idiopathomechanism of vitiligo: a convergance theory. *Experimental Dermatology, 2*: 145–153.

Lefebvre, A., Travis, F., Arndt, E.M. and Munro, I.R. (1986). A psychiatric profile before and after reconstructive surgery in children with Apert's syndrome. *British Journal of Plastic Surgery, 39*: 510–513.

Lerner, A.B., and Nordlund, J.J. (1974). In Porter, J.R., Beuf, A.H., Lerner, A. and Nordlund, J. (1990). The effect of vitiligo on sexual relationships. *Journal of the American Academy of Dermatology, 22*: 221–222.

Lloyd, M. and Bor, R. (1996) *Communication Skills for Medicine.* Edinburgh: Churchill Livingstone.

MacAlpine, I. (1958). A critical evaluation of psychosomatic medicine in relation to dermatology. In McKenna, R.M.B (ed.), *Modern Trends in Dermatology*, 2nd series. London: Buttterworth.

Malt, U. (1980). Long term psychosocial follow-up studies of burned adults: review of the literature. *Burns, 6*: 190–197.

Malt, U. and Ugland, O. (1989). A long-term psychosocial follow-up study of burned adults. *Acta Psychiatra., 355*: 94–102.

Martin, D. (1989). *Counselling and Therapy Skills.* Illinois: Waveland Press Inc.

Mayou, R. (1989). Illness behaviour and psychiatry. *General Hospital Psychiatry, 11*: 307–312.

McDaniel, S., and Campbell, T. (1986). Physicians and family therapists: the risk of collaboration. *Family Systems Medicine, 4*: 4–10.

McDaniel, S., Hepworth, J., and Doherty, W. (1992). *Medical Family Therapy.* New York: Basic Books.

McGregor, F. (1951). Some psycho-social problems associated with facial deformities. *American Sociological Review. 16*: 629–638.

Meehl, P. (1962). Schizotaxia, schizotype, schizophrenia. *American Psychologist. 17*(1): 827–838.

Moss, T., (1997). Individual variation in adjusting to visible differences. In Lansdown, R.L., Rumsey, N., Bradburey, E., Carr, T., and Partridge, J. (eds), (1997) *Visibly Different: Coping with Disfigurement.* Oxford: Butterworth Heinemann.

Ortonne, J.P., Mosher, D.B., and Fitzpatrick, T.B. (1983). *Vitiligo and Other Hypomelanoses of Hair and Skin.* New York: Plenum Medical Books.

Pankova, A. (1991). An examination of autonomic reactivity in a group of dermatology patients. *Acta Dermatologica. 12*(2): 312–316.

Papadopoulos, L., Bor, R., and Legg, C. (1999a). Coping with the disfiguring effects of vitiligo: a preliminary investigation into the effects of cognitive behavioural therapy. *British Journal of Medical Psychology. 72*(3): 385–396.

Papadopoulos, L., Bor, R., and Legg, C. (1999b). Psychological factors in cutaneous disease: A review. *Psychological, Health and Medicine. 4*(2): 107–126.

Papadopoulos, L., Bor, R., Legg, C., and Hawk, J. (1998). Impact of stressful life events on the onset of vitiligo in adults: preliminary evidence for a psychological dimension in aetiology. *Clinical and Experimental Dermatology, 23*(6): 243–248.

Patterson, D., Everrett, J. and Bombardier, C. (1993). Psychological effects of severe burn injuries. *Psychological Bulletin, 113*: 362–378.

Porter, J.R., and Beuf, A.H. (1994). The effect of racially consonant medical context on adjustment of African American patients to physical disability. *Medical Anthropology, 16*: (1): 1–16.

Porter, J.R., Beuf, A.H., Lerner, A. and Nordlund, J. (1990). The effect of vitiligo on sexual relationships. *Journal of the American Academy of Dermatology, 22*: 221–222.

Porter, J.R., Beuf. A., Lerner, A., Nordlund, J. (1986). Psychosocial effects of vitiligo: a comparison of vitiligo patients with 'normal' controls, with psoriasis patients and with patients with other pigment disorders. *Journal of the American Academy of Dermatology. 15*: 220–224.

Porter, J.R., Beuf. A., Lerner, A., Nordlund, J. (1987). Response to cosmetic disfigurement: patients with vitiligo. *Cutis. 39*: 493–494.

Robinson, E., (1997). Psychological research on visible difference in adults. In Lansdown, R. et al. *Visibly Different, Coping with Disfigurement*. Oxford: Butterworth Heinemann.

Robinson, E., Rumsey, N. and Partridge J. (1996). An evaluation of the impact of social interaction skills training for facially disfigured people. *British Journal of Plastic Surgery, 49*: 281–289.

Rogers, C.R. (1961). *On Becoming a Person*. Boston: Houghton Mifflin.

Rolland, J. (1994). *Families, Illness and Disability*. New York: Basic Books.

Root, S., Kent, G. and Al'Abadie, M.S.K. (1994). Disease severity disability and stress in patients undergoing PUVA treatment for psoriasis. *Dermatology, 189*(3): 234–237.

Rudzki, E., Borkowski, W. and Czulbaski, K. (1970) The suggestive effect of placebo the intensity of chronic urticaria. *Acta Allergol, 25*: 70–73.

Salzer, B.A and Schallreuter, K.U. (1995). Investigation of the personality structure in patients with vitiligo and a possible association with impaired catecholamine metabolism. *Dermatology, 190*: 109–115.

Schoenberg, B. and Car, A.C. (1963). An investigation of criteria for brief psychotherapy of neurodermatitis. *Psychosomatic Medicine, 253*–263.

Shaw, W.C. (1981). Folklore surrounding facial deformity and the origins of facial prejudice. *British Journal of Plastic Surgery, 34*: 237–246.

Sheridan, C.L. and Radmacher, S.A. (1991). *Health Psychology: Challenging the Biomedical Model*. John Wiley and Sons:New York.

Sigelman, C.K., Miller, T.E. and Whitworth, L.A. (1986). The early development of stigmatizing reactions to physical differences. *Journal of Applied Developmental Psychology, 7*: 17–32.

Stokes, J.H., Kulchar, G.V. and Pillsbury, D.M. (1945). Effect on the skin of nervous and emotional states. As cited in Whitlock, F.A. (1976). *Psychophysiological Aspects of Skin Disease*. London: W.B Saunders Limited.

Surman, O.S., Gottlieb, S.K., Hackett, T.P. and Silverberg, E.L. (1973). Hypnosis in the treatment of warts. *Archives of General Psychiatry, 28*: 439–441.

Teshima, H., Kubo, C., Kohara, H., Imada, Y., Ago, Y. and Ikemi, Y. (1982). Psychosomatic aspects of skin disease from the standpoint of immunology. *Psychotherapy and Psychosomatics, 37*(3): 165–175.

Teshima, H., Nagata, S., Kinara, H., Sogawa, H., and Ago, Y. (1986). Psychobiological studies on the onset of allergic disease: a Japanese approach. *Advances, 3*(4): 143–149.

Timberlake, E.M. (1985). Self concept protection by children with physical differences. *Child and Adolescent Social Work Journal*, 2(4): 232–246.

Tuke, D.H. (1884). Influence of the mind upon the body. In: Whitlock, F.A. (1976). *Psychophysiological Aspects of Skin Disease*. London: W.B Saunders Limited.

Turk, D. and Salovey, P. (1996). Cognitive behavioural treatment of illness behaviour. In Nicassio, P. and Smith, T. (eds), *Managing Chronic Illness: A Biopsychosocial Perspective*. Washington DC: APA Press.

Watzlawick, P., Weakland, J. and Fisch, R. (1974). *Change: Principles of Problem Formation and Problem Resolution*. New York: W.W. Norton.

Waxman, D. (1974). Behaviour therapy for psoriasis. *Postgraduate Medical Journal,*. 49: 591–592.

Whitlock, F.A. (1976). *Psychophysiological Aspects of Skin Disease*. London: W.B Saunders Limited.

Williams, T. and Griffiths, E. (1991) Psychological consequences of burn injury. *Burns*, 17(6): 478–480.

Wilson, A. (1863). As cited in Whitlock, F.A. (1976). *Psychophysiological Aspects of Skin Disease*. London: W.B Saunders Limited.

Winkler, F. (1911). Ueber der Pruritus cutaneous universalis. In Whitlock, F.A. (1976). *Psychophysiological Aspects of Skin Disease*. London: W.B Saunders Limited.

Wolpe, J. (1980). Behaviour therapy for psychosomatic disorders. *Psychosomatics*, 21: 379–385.

Woodruff, P.W.R., Higgens, E.M., duVivier, A.W.P. and Wessley, S. (1997). Psychiatric illness in patients referred to a dermatology-psychiatry clinic. *General Hospital Psychiatry*, 19(1): 29–35.

Wright, L., Watson, W., and Bell, J. (1996). *Beliefs: The Heart of Healing in Families and Illness*. New York: Basic Books.

Appendix 1a: Psoriasis Disability Index

Thank you for your help in completing this questionnaire. Please could you note the following points.

1. Every question relates to the **LAST FOUR WEEKS ONLY.**

2. Every question should be answered by ringing one of the numbers from 0–6. '0' represents 'not at all' and '6' represents 'very much'. The other numbers represent grades between these two extremes.

3. There are two different versions of questions 6, 7 and 8. If you are **at regular work or at school,** please answer the first batch of questions **6–8.** If you are **not at work or school,** please answer the alternative questions on page 2.

4. Please note that there are 15 questions. **Please check that you have answered all the questions** on the three pages.

All questions relate to the LAST FOUR WEEKS.

DAILY ACTIVITIES:

1. How much has your psoriasis interfered with you carrying out work around the house or garden?

Not at all   = 0   1   2   3   4   5   6 = **Very much**

2. How often have you worn different types or colours of clothes because of your psoriasis?

Not at all   = 0   1   2   3   4   5   6 = **Very much**

3. How much more have you had to change or wash your clothes?

Not at all   = 0   1   2   3   4   5   6 = **Very much**

4. How much of a problem has your psoriasis been at the hairdressers?

Not at all   = 0   1   2   3   4   5   6 = **Very much**

5. How much has your psoriasis resulted in you having to take more baths than usual?

Not at all   = 0   1   2   3   4   5   6 = **Very much**

WORK OR SCHOOL (if appropriate):

6. How much has your psoriasis made you lose time off work or school over the last four weeks?

Not at all = **0** **1** **2** **3** **4** **5** **6** = **Very much**

7. How much has your psoriasis prevented you from doing things at work or school over the last four weeks?

Not at all = **0** **1** **2** **3** **4** **5** **6** = **Very much**

8. Has your career been affected by your psoriasis? e.g. promotion refused, lost a job, asked to change a job.

Not at all = **0** **1** **2** **3** **4** **5** **6** = **Very much**

IF NOT AT WORK OR SCHOOL: Alternative Questions

6. How much has your psoriasis **stopped you** carrying out your normal daily activities over the last four weeks?

Not at all = **0** **1** **2** **3** **4** **5** **6** = **Very much**

7. How much has your psoriasis **altered the way** in which you carry out your normal daily activities over the last four weeks?

Not at all = **0** **1** **2** **3** **4** **5** **6** = **Very much**

8. Has your career been affected by your psoriasis? e.g. promotion refused, lost a job, asked to change a job.

Not at all = **0** **1** **2** **3** **4** **5** **6** = **Very much**

PERSONAL RELATIONSHIPS:

9. Has your psoriasis resulted in sexual difficulties over the last four weeks?

Not at all = **0** **1** **2** **3** **4** **5** **6** = **Very much**

10. Has your psoriasis created problems with your partner or any of your close friends or relatives?

Not at all = **0** **1** **2** **3** **4** **5** **6** = **Very much**

LEISURE:

11. How much has your psoriasis stopped you going out socially or to any special functions?

Not at all = **0** **1** **2** **3** **4** **5** **6** = **Very much**

12.   Is your psoriasis making it difficult for you to do any sport?

Not at all   = 0   1   2   3   4   5   6 = Very much

13. Have you been unable to use, criticized or stopped from using communal
     bathing or changing facilities?

Not at all   = 0   1   2   3   4   5   6 = Very much

14. Has your psoriasis resulted in you smoking or drinking alcohol more than
     you would do normally?

Not at all   = 0   1   2   3   4   5   6 = Very much

TREATMENT:

15. To what extent has your psoriasis or treatment made your home messy or
     untidy?

Not at all   = 0   1   2   3   4   5   6 = Very much

Thank you for your help.

Source: Finlay A.Y., Khan G.K., Luscombe D.K., Salek M.S. Validation of sick-
ness impact profile and Psoriasis Disability Index in psoriasis. *British Journal of
Dermatology*, 1990, 123: 751–756

Appendix 1b: Dermatitis Family Impact Questionnaire

Child's Name: Mother/Father/Carer   Date: Score

The aim of this Questionnaire is to measure how much your child's skin problem has affected you and your family OVER THE LAST WEEK. Please tick one box for each question.

1. Over the *last week* how much effect has your child having eczema had on **housework**, e.g. washing, cleaning?

    Very much   ☐
    A lot   ☐
    A little   ☐
    Not at all   ☐

2. Over the *last week* how much effect has your child having eczema had on **food preparation** and **feeding**?

    Very much   ☐
    A lot   ☐
    A little   ☐
    Not at all   ☐

3. Over the *last week* how much effect has your child having eczema had on the **sleep of others in family**?

    Very much   ☐
    A lot   ☐
    A little   ☐
    Not at all   ☐

4. Over the *last week* how much effect has your child having eczema had on **family leisure activities**, e.g. swimming?

    Very much   ☐
    A lot   ☐
    A little   ☐
    Not at all   ☐

5. Over the *last week* how much effect has your child having eczema had on **time spent on shopping for the family?**

Very much ☐
A lot ☐
A little ☐
Not at all ☐

6. Over the *last week* how much effect has your child having eczema had on your **expenditure,** e.g. costs related to treatment, clothes, etc?

Very much ☐
A lot ☐
A little ☐
Not at all ☐

7. Over the *last week* how much effect has your child having eczema had on causing **tiredness** or **exhaustion** in your child's parents/carers?

Very much ☐
A lot ☐
A little ☐
Not at all ☐

8. Over the *last week* how much effect has your child having eczema had on causing **emotional distress** such as depression, frustration or guilt in your child's parents/carers?

Very much ☐
A lot ☐
A little ☐
Not at all ☐

9. Over the *last week* how much effect has your child having eczema had on **relationships** between the **main carer and partner** or between the **main carer and other children** in the family?

Very much ☐
A lot ☐
A little ☐
Not at all ☐

10. Over the *last week* how much effect has **helping with your child's treatment** had on the main carer's life?

Very much   ☐
A lot   ☐
A little   ☐
Not at all   ☐

Please check you have answered EVERY question. Thank you

Souce: Lawson, V., Lewis-Jones, M. S., Finlay, A.Y., Reid, P., Owens, R.G., The family impact of childhood atopic dermatitis: the Dermatitis Family Impact questionnaire. *British Journal of Dermatology*, 1998; *138*: 107–113.

Appendix 1c: Children's Life Quality Index

Hospital No:
Name: **Date:**   Score:
Address: **Diagnosis:**
dob:

The aim of this questionnaire is to measure how much your child has been affected by their health problem OVER THE LAST THREE MONTHS. Please tick one box for each question.

1. Over the last three months, how much has your child's health problem resulted in **tiredness, lack of energy** or **changes in mood**?

    Very much ☐
    A lot ☐
    A little ☐
    Not at all ☐

2. Over the last three months, how much has your child's health problem resulted in **difficult behaviour**?

    Very much ☐
    A lot ☐
    A little ☐
    Not at all ☐

3. Over the last three months, how much has your child's health problem resulted in **any pain**?

    Very much ☐
    A lot ☐
    A little ☐
    Not at all ☐

4. Over the last three months, how much has your child's health problem resulted in **sleep** (e.g. waking or coughing)?

    Very much ☐
    A lot ☐
    A little ☐
    Not at all ☐

5. Over the last three months, how much has your child's health problem resulted in **lack of appetite** or **diet restrictions**?

   Very much ☐
   A lot ☐
   A little ☐
   Not at all ☐

6. Over the last three months, how much has your child's health problem resulted in problems with or restrictions of **games, sports** or **playing**?

   Very much ☐
   A lot ☐
   A little ☐
   Not at all ☐

7. Over the last three months, how much has your child's health problem affected **meeting friends** or **going out with family**?

   Very much ☐
   A lot ☐
   A little ☐
   Not at all ☐

8. Over the last three months, how much has your child's health problem resulted in others calling the child **names, teasing, bullying** or asking **questions** or giving **unwanted attention**?

   Very much ☐
   A lot ☐
   A little ☐
   Not at all ☐

9. Over the last three months, how much has your child's health problem resulted in **missing school time**?

   Very much ☐
   A lot ☐
   A little ☐
   Not at all ☐

10. Over the last three months, how much has your child's health problem **affected school work** or **progress** in school?

Very much ☐
A lot ☐
A little ☐
Not at all ☐

11. Over the last three months, how much has your child's health problem resulted in a need for frequent **visits** to the **doctor** or **hospital**?

Very much ☐
A lot ☐
A little ☐
Not at all ☐

12. Over the last three months, how much has your child's health problem resulted in a need for frequent **treatment at home**, (e.g. injections, medication or physiotherapy)?

Very much ☐
A lot ☐
A little ☐
Not at all ☐

© M. S. Lewis-Jones, A. Y. Finlay 1995. This questionnaire is reproduced by permission of the authors. For permission to reproduce this questionnaire please contact Dr A Y Finlay, Department of Dermatology, University of Wales College of Medicine, Heath Park, Cardiff CF4 4XN, UK.

Source: Lewis-Jones, M.S., Finlay, A.Y,. The Children's Dermatology Life Quality Index (CDLQI): Initial validation and practical use, *British Journal of Dermatology*, 1995; *132*: 942–949.

Appendix 1d: Dermatology Life Quality Index

Hospital No: Date:

Name: Score:

Address: Diagnosis:

The aim of this questionnaire is to measure how much your skin problem has affected your life OVER THE LAST WEEK. Please tick one box for each question.

1. Over the last week, how **itchy, sore, painful** or **stinging** has your skin been?

    Very much ☐
    A lot ☐
    A little ☐
    Not at all ☐

2. Over the last week, how **embarrassed** or **self-conscious** have you been because of your skin?

    Very much ☐
    A lot ☐
    A little ☐
    Not at all ☐

3. Over the last week, how much has your skin interfered with you going **shopping** or looking after your **home** or **garden**?

    Very much ☐
    A lot ☐
    A little ☐
    Not at all ☐
    Not relevant ☐

4. Over the last week, how much has your skin influenced the **clothes** you wear?

    Very much ☐
    A lot ☐
    A little ☐
    Not at all ☐
    Not relevant ☐

5. Over the last week, how much has your skin affected any **social** or **leisure** activities?

    Very much ☐
    A lot ☐
    A little ☐
    Not at all ☐
    Not relevant ☐

6. Over the last week, how much has your skin made it difficult for you to do any **sport**?

    Very much ☐
    A lot ☐
    A little ☐
    Not at all ☐
    Not relevant ☐

7. Over the last week, has your skin prevented you from **working** or **studying**? If 'no', over the last week how much has your skin been a problem at **work** or **studying**?

    Very much ☐
    A lot ☐
    A little ☐
    Not at all ☐
    Not relevant ☐

8. Over the last week, how much has your skin created problems with your **partner** or any of your **close friends** or **relatives?**

    Very much ☐
    A lot ☐
    A little ☐
    Not at all ☐
    Not relevant ☐

9. Over the last week, how much has your skin caused any **sexual difficulties**?

Very much ☐
A lot ☐
A little ☐
Not at all ☐
Not relevant ☐

10. Over the last week, how much of a problem has the **treatment** for your skin been, for example by making your home messy, or by taking up time?

Very much ☐
A lot ☐
A little ☐
Not at all ☐
Not relevant ☐

Source: Finlay, A.Y., Khan, G.K., Dermatology Life Quality Index (DLQI): a simple pracatical measure for routine clinical use, *Clinical and Experimental Dermatology*, 1994; *19*: 210–216.

Appendix 1e: The Acne Disability Questionnaire

1. As a result of having acne, during the last month have you been aggressive, frustrated or embarrassed?

   (a) Very much indeed ☐
   (b) A lot ☐
   (c) A little ☐
   (d) Not at all ☐

2. Do you think that having acne during the last month interfered with your daily social life, social events or relationships with members of the opposite sex?

   (a) Severely, affecting all activities ☐
   (b) Moderately, in most activities ☐
   (c) Occasionally or only in some activities ☐
   (d) Not at all ☐

3. During the last month have you avoided public changing facilities or wearing swimming costumes because of your acne?

   (a) All of the time ☐
   (b) Most of the time ☐
   (c) Occasionally ☐
   (d) Not at all ☐

4. How would you describe your feelings about the appearance of your skin over the last month?

   (a) Very depressed and miserable ☐
   (b) Usually concerned ☐
   (c) Occasionally concerned ☐
   (d) Not bothered ☐

5. Please indicate how bad you think your acne is now:

   (a) The worst it could possibly be ☐
   (b) A major problem ☐
   (c) A minor problem ☐
   (d) Not a problem ☐

Source: Motley, R.J., Finlay, A.Y., Practical use of a disability index in the routine management of acne, *Clinical and Experimental Dermatology*, 1992; 17:1–3.

List of Organizations

Acne Support Group
PO Box 230
Hayes
UB4 OUT
Middlesex

Behcet's Syndrome Society
3 Church Close
Lambourn
Hungerford
RG17 8PU
Berks

British Allergy Foundation
Deepdene House
30 Bellegrove Road
Welling
Kent
DA15 3PY

British Association of Cancer
United Patients (BACUP)
3 Bath Place
Rivington Street
London
EC2A 3JR

British Red Cross
9 Grosvenor Crescent
London
SW1X 7EJ

Changing Faces
1 & 2 Junction Mews
Paddington
London
W2 1PN

Darier's Disease Support Group
PO Box 36
Milford Haven
Dyfed
SA73 3YF

Dystrophic Epidermiolysis Bullosa
Research Association
Debra House
13 Wellington Business Park
Dukes Ride
Crowthorne
RG45 6LS

Ehlers-Danlos Support Group
1 Chandler Close
Richmond
North Yorks
DL10 5QQ

Hairline International
Lyons Court
1668 High Street
Knowle
West Midlands
B93 OLY

The Herpes Viruses Association
41 North Road
London
N7 9DP

Hodgkin's Disease & Lymphoma
Association
PO Box 275
Haddenham
Aylesbury
Bucks
HP17 8JJ

In Touch Trust
10 Norman Road
Cheshire
M33 3DF

Latex Allergy Support Group
PO Box 36
Cheltenham
GL52 3WY

LEPRA - The British Leprosy
Relief Association
Fairfax House
Causton Road
Colchester
Essex
CD1 1PU

Let's Face It
14 Fallowfield
Yateley
Hampshire
GU46 6LV

Let's Face It
62 Fortescue Road
Edgware
Middlesex
HA8 OHN

Lupus UK
James House
Eastern Road
Romford
Essex
RM1 3NH

Marc's Line (Melanoma and
Related Cancers of the Skin)
Dermatology Treatment Centre
Salisbury District Hospital
Salisbury
Wiltshire
SP2 BBJ

Marfan Association UK
Rochester House
5 Aldershot Road
Fleet
Hampshire
GU13 9NG

National Eczema Society
163 Eversholt Street
London
NW1 1BU

The Neurofibromatosis
Association
82 London Road
Kingston upon Thames
Surrey
KT2 6PX

The Pemphigus Vulgaris Network
Flat C
26 St Germaine Road
London
SE23 1RJ

The Pseudoxanthoma Elasticum
(PXE) Support Group
15 Mead Close
Marlow
Bucks
SL7 1HR

Primary Immunodeficiency
Association (PIA)
Alliance House
12 Caxton Street
London
SW1H OQS

The Psoriasis Association
Milton House
7 Milton Street
Northampton
NN2 7JG

Psoriatic Arthropathy Alliance
PO Box 111
St Albans
Herts
AL2 3JO

Raynaud's & Scleroderma
Association Trust
112 Crewe Road
Alsagor
Cheshire
ST7 2JA

Shingles Support Society
41 North Road
London
N7 9DP

Telangiegtasia Self Help Group
39 Sunny Croft
Downley
High Wycombe
Bucks
HP13 5UQ

Terence Higgins Trust
62–64 Gray's Inn Road
London
WC1X 8JU

Tuberous Sclerosis Association
Little Barnsley Farm
Catshill
Bromsgrove
Worcester
B61 ONQ

The Vitiligo Society
125 Kennington Road
London
SE116SF

All Party Parliamentary Group on
Skin
3/19 Holmbush Road
London
SW15 3LE

Glossary

[Items indicated in bold in the text.]

Acute illness: a condition that occurs over a short period of time and is reversible.

Albinism: a rare inherited disorder in which the pigment-producing cells (melanocytes) are present but do not produce pigment. People who have the disorder tend to have white hair, very pale skin and pink eyes.

Atopic diseases: as a rule people who suffer from atopic diseases such as asthma or atopic eczema have an inherited predisposition to become allergic to substances that are harmless to people who are not atopic.

Autoimmune disorder: disorders where the immune system falsely recognizes and attacks its own healthy tissue.

Body image: one's perception of one's physical appearance and physical functioning.

Chorionic villus sampling (CVS): a prenatal technique used in the first trimester of pregnancy in order to detect fetal abnormalities.

Cognitive distortions: systematic errors in reasoning that exert a negative influence on a person's general functioning. They often manifest as irrational or negative perceptions of oneself, the future and one's current circumstances.

Cognitive restructuring: a procedure through which negative or erroneous thought patterns are modified in adaptive ways.

Congenital abnormalities: physical or mental defects that are present at birth.

Cyst: a solid elevation of skin filled with fluid or semi-solid material.

Excoriation: a crusted area of skin caused by scratching, rubbing or picking.

Humanism: the view that every person has within them the potential for personal growth and self-actualization.

Iatrogenic: an illness or disease caused by the treatment of another medical illness.

Naevus: a benign proliferation of skin cells; melanocytic (also known as mole) is one of the most common forms.

Nodule: a small (10mm) palpable solid lesion that can involve any layer of the skin and may or may not be elevated.

Papule: a small (5mm) sold elevated lesion of the skin.

Psychoneuroimmunology: the study of the reciprocal influences between the immune system and psychological states and the neurological system.

Pustule: a superficial, visible collection of pus in a blister.

Sebaceous glands: associated with hair follicles, especially those of the face, scalp and back; small during childhood but become larger and active during puberty.

Sebum: oily substance produced by the sebaceous glands, the function of which is uncertain.

Self-concept: an integrated set of beliefs regarding personal attributes and qualities.

Skin biopsy: a process whereby a portion of a skin lesion is removed and studied hystologically in order to establish or confirm a diagnosis.

Vascular disorder: involving arteries, veins or lymphatics, often cause intracutaneous haemorrhaging, resulting in small and large bruises.

Index

Note:
Page numbers in **bold** type refer to **figures**
Page numbers in *italic* type refer to *tables*
Page numbers followed by 'B' refer to boxes eg 21B